THE
CHINESE KINSHIP SYSTEM

Han-yi Fêng [Fêng Han-chi]

PUBLISHED FOR THE HARVARD-YENCHING INSTITUTE
BY THE HARVARD UNIVERSITY PRESS
CAMBRIDGE, MASSACHUSETTS
1948

Reprinted from the *Harvard Journal of Asiatic Studies*
Vol. II, No. 2 (July, 1937), pp. 141ff.

THE CHINESE KINSHIP SYSTEM

Han-yi Fêng [Fêng Han-chi]
Harvard University

CONTENTS	PAGE
Foreword	2
Abbreviations	2
Definition of terms	2
Chronology	2
Introduction	4
Principles of Terminological Composition	8
Nuclear Terms	8
Basic Modifiers	10
Terminological Composition	11
Referential Modifiers	13
Vocative Terms	17
Supernumerary Terms	19
Structural Principles and Terminological Categories	20
Lineal and Collateral Differentiation	20
Generation Stratification	24
Categories	27
Reciprocity	30
Factors Affecting the System	32
The Sib: Decent and Exogamy	33
Mourning Grades	38
Cross-cousin Marriage	43
Sororate	46
Levirate	51
Teknonymy	54
Historical Review of Terms	64
Consanguineal Relatives:	67
Relatives through father—Table I	67
Relatives through mother—Table II	107
Affinal Relatives	114
Relatives through wife—Table III	114
Relatives through husband—Table IV	121
Conclusions	126
Chinese Works Frequently Cited	130

FOREWORD

ABBREVIATIONS

e = ego
f = father, father's
m = mother, mother's
s = son, son's
d = daughter, daughter's
b = brother, brother's
si = sister, sister's

h = husband, husband's
w = wife, wife's
o = older
y = younger
> = older than
< = younger than

Example: m f b s d > e signifies mother's father's brother's son's daughter older than ego.

DEFINITION OF TERMS

All terms are used in their customary meanings, as found in anthropological and sociological literature. A few terms are used here with a specialized connotation in connection with the Chinese social system. They are the following:

Family: used always in the sense of the "extended family" or the *Gross-Familie*, and equivalent to the Chinese term *chia* 家, or *chia ting* 家庭.

Sib: a group of people possessing a common sibname (patronym), descended from a common male ancestor, no matter how remote, and characterized by a feeling of relationship. Descent is strictly patrilineal, and the group is strictly exogamous. An organization for the common welfare of all its members, and ancestor "worship," may or may not be present. It is equivalent to the Chinese term, *tsung tsu* 宗族.

Sibname: used in the sense of a patronym or surname which all members of a sib possess in common, and equivalent to the Chinese term *hsing* 姓. Descent of the sibname is strictly patrilineal.

Sib relative: relatives who belong to the same sib and possess the same sibname as ego. It is equivalent to the Chinese term *tsung ch'in* 宗親, or *tsu jên* 族人 "clansmen."

Non-sib relative: relative who belongs to a sib other than ego's and bears a sibname other than ego's. It is equivalent to the Chinese terms *wai ch'in* 外親 and *nei ch'in* 內親 combined; or the old legal term *ch'in shu* 親屬. *Wai ch'in* refers to relatives through women of the sib married out, and the affinal relatives of father, father's father, and ascending. *Nei ch'in* refers to ego's own affinal relatives.

CHRONOLOGY

The following chronology is given for those who are not familiar with Chinese history since it is impossible to give the Western date in every instance. The tripartite division does not correspond to the traditional Chinese historical divisions but has been adopted here simply with reference to the evolution of the kinship system.

FOREWORD

Ancient period: first millennium B. C., which includes the following dynastic periods:

Chou dynasty, or the feudal period, ca. 1100-249 B. C.
Ch'in dynasty, 248-207 B. C.
Former Han dynasty, 206 B. C.-24 A. D.

Transitional period: first millennium A. D., which includes the following dynastic periods:

Later Han dynasty,	25-220 A. D.	
Wei dynasty,	220-264 A. D.	
Chin dynasty,	265-420 A. D.	
Sung dynasty,	420-479 A. D	Northern Wei dynasty, 399-534 A. D.
Ch'i dynasty,	479-502 A. D.	Northern Ch'i dynasty, 550-577 A. D.
Liang dynasty,	502-557 A. D.	
Ch'ên dynasty,	557-589 A. D.	
Sui dynasty,	581-618 A. D.	
T'ang dynasty,	618-907 A. D.	
Wu tai,	907-960 A. D.	

Modern period: second millennium A. D., which includes the following dynastic periods:

Sung dynasty,	960-1279 A. D.	(This is the Sung dynasty to which the
Yüan dynasty,	1280-1368 A. D.	writer will always refer in the present
Ming dynasty,	1368-1644 A. D.	treatise, not to the one mentioned above
Ch'ing dynasty,	1644-1911 A. D.	under 420-479 A. D.)

[Other contemporary dynastic periods are omitted here since they are not referred to in this work.]

Ancient system: system of the ancient period, i. e., the system in the *Êrh Ya*, supplemented by the *I Li*, the *Li Chi*, and other contemporary sources.

Modern system: system of the modern period, i. e., the present Chinese system.

INTRODUCTION

The interest of the Chinese themselves in problems of kinship was manifested quite early. This interest is primarily a practical one, for the whole Chinese social structure is built upon the basis of the " extended family " organization, which in turn is based upon the systematization of the mutual relationships among its members. If the whole social structure is to function harmoniously, the kinship system, which expresses and defines the rights and obligations of individuals to each other, must first be adjusted. This ideology is further fostered by the teachings of Confucianism, so that kinship becomes a subject of perennial interest.

The systematic recording of relationship terms goes back as far as the *Êrh Ya*,[1] a work of the third or second century B. C. (according to the more conservative dating), in which the terms are carefully classified and arranged. Subsequent works of a similar nature all contain special chapters on kinship nomenclature, e. g., the *Shih Ming* [ca. 200 A. D.] and the *Kuang Ya* [ca. 230 A. D.]—to mention only two of the comparatively earlier ones. These works record later terms which are not present in the *Êrh Ya* and in a sense bring the *Êrh Ya* system up to the date of each compilation. This practice has continued down to the present day.[2] Even larger encyclopaedic works devote special sections to this subject, e. g., the *T'ai p'ing yü lan* (983 A. D.)

---

[1] Tradition has it that the *ÊrhYa* was compiled by Chou Kung [?-1105 B. C.] and augmented by Confucius [551-479 B. C.], Tzŭ Hsia 子夏 [507-? B. C.], Shu-sun T'ung 叔孫通 [ca. 200 B. C.] and others. It is not the work of one hand, nor of one period, but developed gradually during the first millennium B. C. Cf. B. KARLGREN, *BMFEA* 3(1931). 44-49. The section on Kinship Terms 釋親 probably dates from ca. 200 B. C. Cf. 爾雅新研究 by NAITŌ Torajirō, in 先秦經籍考 2.163-184.

[2] Most works of the 訓詁 class have a section on kinship terms, e. g., the *P'ien ya* 駢雅 [under 5. 釋名稱], *Shih ya* 拾雅, etc., and even works on dialects like the *Hsü fang yen* 續方言 of HANG Shih-chün 杭世駿 [1696-1773], and the *I yü* 異語 of CH'IEN Tien 錢坫 [1744-1806] devote special sections to kinship term variants. Other dictionaries, starting from the *Shuo wên*, contain kinship terms too, but they are not systematically arranged.

has ten chapters,³ and the *T'u shu chi ch'êng* 112 chapters,⁴ on kinship nomenclature. Naturally, not all this material is relevant, and much of it belongs to *belles lettres*. In the Ch'ing dynasty a series of special works on kinship terms appeared, the most important and extensive of which are the *Ch'êng wei lu* 稱謂錄 of LIANG Chang-chü 梁章鉅 [1775-1849], and the *Ch'in shu chi* 親屬記 of CHÊNG Chên 鄭珍 [1806-1864]. Both of these works comprise collections of old terms, and are more or less in the *Êrh Ya* tradition. Of the two, the *Ch'êng wei lu* is much wider in scope, but the arrangement of material is rather loose. The *Ch'in shu chi* considers only the lineal relatives through father, and the ordering of data is more in keeping with the view of orthodox Confucianism.⁵

By far the most important class of materials is formed by the ritual works, the *Li*. In these works kinship is not treated as a subject by itself but in connection with other subjects; an exception is the *Ch'in shu chi*, a lost section of the *Li*, which dealt primarily with relationship terminology.⁶ These ritual works are important sources for the functional study of the Chinese kinship system because they deal with kinship in action. Such are the *I Li* and the *Li Chi*, works of the second half of the first millenium B. C., that treat kinship *in extenso*, especially in connection with mourning rites, ancestor " worship," and other aspects of ritual. In all later works on ritualism—too numerous to mention here— kinship is the basic subject of discussion.

In addition, there are numerous miscellaneous works in which discussions on kinship terms occasionally occur. These are among the most important sources from the standpoint of the evolution of the Chinese kinship system, because generally it is here that

---

³ 太平御覽, 511-521, 宗親部.
⁴ 圖書集成, 明倫彙編：家範典, 1-112.
⁵ Other important works are the *T'ung su pien* 通俗編 [ch. 4: 倫常, ch. 18: 稱謂] of CHAI Hao 翟灝, ?-1788; the *Hêng yen lu* 恆言錄 [ch. 3: 親屬稱謂類] of CH'IEN Ta-hsin 錢大昕, 1727-1804; the *Chêng su wên* 證俗文 [ch. 4] of Ho I-hsing 郝懿行 1757-1825; and the *Kuang shih ch'in* 廣釋親 of CHANG Shên-i 張慎儀. There are many other works of a less extensive nature but they rather duplicate each other.
⁶ As quoted in *Pai hu t'ung* 8.19b, the *Ch'in shu chi* 親屬記 is very similar in nature to the *Êrh Ya*.

one finds recorded the newly introduced terms (dialectical or unconventional) which, as a rule, are ignored by the ritual and other formal literature. Very often one finds in them enlightening discussions concerning the introduction and origin of new terminologies.

Thus, the interest in the study of kinship terminology is not new among Chinese scholars, and actually they sometimes made explanations which might rank with modern sociological interpretations, but the systematic socio-anthropological study began with Lewis H. Morgan.[7] Morgan's data were supplied by Robert Hart, an Englishman in the employ of the Chinese Maritime Customs. Despite the faulty nature of Hart's material, and notwithstanding Morgan's evolutionistic predilections, which invalidated most of his conclusions, the Morgan-Hart work has remained the basis for most subsequent speculation. Since then has appeared a number of miscellaneous recordings, some in legal treatises or linguistic primers, others in lexicographic works, but, with one exception, none is worthy of serious consideration. This exception is the work of T. S. Chen and J. K. Shryock.[8] The Chen-Shryock study is based chiefly on two modern dictionaries, the *Tz'ŭ yüan* and the *Chung hua ta tzŭ tien*. This material, although inadequate and unreliable, has been used to good advantage by the authors. George W. Bounakoff [9] seems to have made a stupendous attempt to synthesize all the material in European languages in the light of Morgan's hypothesis.

---

[7] *Systems of Consanguinity and Affinity of the Human Family*, 1870, Part III, ch. IV. 413-437.

[8] "Chinese Relationship Terms," *American Anthropologist* 34 (1932). 623-664.

[9] *Terms of Relationship in Chinese: An Ethnographical-Linguistic Study* [N. J. Marr Institute of Language and Mentality, Academy of Sciences, USSR, 1936]. I have not seen the original work (in Russian) but only the English "Analytical Summary." So far as I can make out, it is mainly based on secondary English sources with the exception of *Êrh Ya*, which is also available in English. Although he has used most of the European sources, he seems to have overlooked the tables of Gustave SCHLEGEL: *Nederlandsch-Chineesch woordenboek met de transcriptie der Chineesche karackters in het Tsiang-tsiu dialekt*, Leiden, 1886-90, vol. I, p. 1343, *Chineesche Geslachtboon*. The important issue, however, is his methodology which is based upon the Marxian conception of history and the Japhetic theory of language of H. I. Marr. Combining these with the evolutionary stages of L. H. Morgan, he arrives at the "collective beginnings" of Chinese society!

The limitations of all these European works are obvious. First, the terms relied upon have been collected by untrained persons from " uninformed " informants. Secondly, the writers have not made use of the vast amount of easily available Chinese documentary material—indeed, they seem unaware of the existence of such material. Consequently, most of these studies are marred by numerous inconsistencies and errors. The writers could seldom determine the exact nature of a term, because few ever sectioned out the multiple strata of terminology in the Chinese system.[10]

The present study is based chiefly upon the author's own collection of terms from the primary Chinese sources. All material consulted has been examined critically to insure correctness in terminology and interpretation. The method of approach is primarily historical and linguistic [11]—partly because it is precisely these aspects which are the most engaging characteristics of the Chinese system and at the same time the least understood, partly because preliminary work of this sort is prerequisite to an understanding of the more implicit aspects of the system. The field of investigation is limited to the historical period, approximately the last twenty-five centuries, within which the system has been fully documented. If kinship system changes occur at all, two thousand years should be long enough for their manifestation.[12]

---

[10] Originally the present work included a section called " Critical Review of Early Studies." As it was not in a way constructive and occupied considerable space, it has been deleted.

[11] By *linguistic*, I mean the usual and the formal approach to the study of kinship systems, i. e., by an examination of the kinship terms themselves, the structural whole they present, and the underlying principles involved.

[12] This paper is one of the studies made by the author under a fellowship grant by the Trustees of the Harvard-Yenching Institute, to whom he wishes to express his gratitude. The author is also deeply indebted to Professors A. I. Hallowell, F. G. Speck, and D. S. Davidson for constant guidance, suggestions and improvements in this work; to Prof. C. K. M. Kluckhohn and Dr. C. M. Arensberg for their careful examination and corrections of the MS.; to Mr. Paul K. Benedict, who has made improvements and corrections on almost every page. The author also wishes to thank Professors S. Elisséeff and J. R. Ware for suggestions and assistance and especially for sponsoring publication in this Journal.

PRINCIPLES OF TERMINOLOGICAL COMPOSITION

The principles governing the composition of terms are both linguistic and sociological. Linguistically, they are formed according to the syntactical principles of the Chinese language; sociologically, their connotations are determined by the relationships which they express and the circumstances under which they are used. The multitude of Chinese relationship terms can be reduced to four fundamental classes, namely, *nuclear terms, basic modifiers, referential modifiers*, and *vocatives*. Nuclear terms express the nuclear group of relationships and, linguistically, are independent of modifiers. Each nuclear term possesses a primary meaning and one or more secondary meanings. The primary meaning is assumed when the term is used independently, and, when it is used in combination with other elements, the secondary meaning or meanings become paramount. Basic modifiers for the most part express collateral relationship and generation status and cannot be used independently as kinship terms. The nuclear terms form the basis for kinship extensions and the basic modifiers locate the exact place of the relative in the total scheme. The combinations and recombinations of these two classes of elements constitute the modern standard system which is the norm of all other terminologies. The referential modifiers modify the standard system into proper forms for referential use in specific applications. Vocatives, aside from their primary usages, transform them into direct forms of address between relatives.

The following is an analysis of these four classes of elements and an exposition of the principles governing their composition and application. In the analysis of the nuclear terms the primary connotations (according to the modern standard system) are given first and then followed by the secondary meanings.

NUCLEAR TERMS

Tsu 祖:[2] Father's father. Ancestor. Used in combination with other elements for all ascendants higher than the father's generation.

Sun 孫:[3] Son's son. Descendant. Used in combination with other elements for all descendants lower than the son's generation.

PRINCIPLES OF TERMINOLOGICAL COMPOSITION

Fu 父:[4] Father. Male of higher generation status. Male sex indicator for higher generations. Suffixed to terms of all male relatives of generations higher than ego.

Tzǔ 子:[5] Son. Male of lower generation status. Male sex indicator for lower generations. May be suffixed to terms of male relatives of generations lower than ego, but its use is optional.

Mu 母:[6] Mother. Female of higher generation status. Female sex indicator for higher generations. Suffixed to terms of all married female relatives of generations higher than ego.

Nü 女:[7] Daughter. Female of lower generation status. Female sex indicator for lower generations. Suffixed to terms of all female relatives of generations lower than ego.

Hsiung 兄:[8] Older brother. Male of the older brother's status. Indicator of seniority within the generation of ego. Used in combination with other elements for male relatives of the generation of, but older than, ego.

Ti 弟:[9] Younger brother. Male of younger brother's status. Indicator of juniority for males within the generation of ego. Used in combination with other elements for male relatives of the generation of, but younger than, ego.

Tzǔ 姊:[10] Older sister. Female of the older sister's status. Indicator of seniority for females within the same generation of ego. Used in combination with other elements for female relatives of the generation of, but older than, ego.

Mei 妹:[11] Younger sister. Female of the younger sister's status. Indicator of juniority for females within the same generation of ego. Used in combination with other elements for female relatives of the generation of, but younger than, ego.

Po 伯:[12] Father's older brother. Indicator of seniority. Applicable to terms from ego's generation and ascending, using the direct male lineal line as a standard of comparison.

Husband's older brother. Cannot be extended in this sense.

Shu 叔:[13] Father's younger brother. Indicator of juniority. Applicable to terms from ego's generation and ascending, using the direct lineal line as a standard of comparison.

Husband's younger brother. Cannot be extended in this last sense.

Chih 姪:[13a] Brother's son. Indicator of descent from male collaterals. Used in combination with other elements for descendants of male relatives of the generation of ego.

Shêng 甥:[14] Sister's son. Indicator of descent from female collaterals. Used in combination with other elements for descendants from female relatives of the generation of ego.

Ku 姑:[15] Father's sister. Indicator of relationship comparable with father's sister's. Indicator of descent from father's sister, or from female relatives comparable with father's sister's relationship.

Husband's sister. Cannot be extended in this last sense.

Chiu 舅:[16] Mother's brother. Indicator of relationship comparable with mother's brother's. Indicator of descent from mother's brother, or from male relatives comparable with mother's brother's relationship.

Wife's brother. Cannot be extended in this last sense.

I 姨: Mother's sister. Indicator of relationship comparable with mother's sister's. Indicator of descent from mother's sister, or from female relatives comparable with mother's sister's relationship. Wife's sister.[17] Indicator of relationship comparable with wife's sister's. Indicator of descent from wife's sister, or from female relatives comparable with wife's sister's relationship.

Yo 岳:[17a] Wife's parents. Indicator of relationship comparable with wife's parents, such as their cousins.

Hsü 婿:[18] Daughter's husband. Husband. Indicator of connection by marriage with ego's female relatives of the same generation of ego and descending.

Fu 夫:[19] ego's husband. Husband. Indicator of connection by marriage with ego's female relatives of the same generation of ego.

Ch'i 妻:[20] ego's wife. Wife.

Sao 嫂:[21] Older brother's wife. Female of older brother's wife's status. Indicator of connection by marriage with ego's male relatives of the generation of, but older than, ego.

Fu 婦:[22] Son's wife. Wife. Indicator of connection by marriage with ego's male relatives of the generation of, but younger than, ego and descending generations.

Basic Modifiers

Kao 高: High; revered. Modifying indicator of the fourth ascending generation.

Tsêng 曾: Added; increased. Modifying indicator for the third ascending and descending generations.

Hsüan 玄: Far; distant. Modifying indicator for the fourth descending generation.

T'ang 堂: Hall; the ancestral hall. Modifying indicator for the second collateral line from the second generation and descending. Ascending vertically, for father's father's brother's children and father's father's father's brother's children, that is, for paternal uncles and aunts once removed and paternal granduncles and aunts once removed. When extended to non-sib relatives, it indicates, in a similar way, the third collateral line.

Ts'ung 從: To follow; through. It is used synonymously with *t'ang*. *T'ang* is a later term and its use is restricted. Wherever *t'ang* is used, *ts'ung* may be substituted, but not vice versa.

Tsai-ts'ung 再從: To follow again, or to follow a second time. Modifying indicator for the third collateral line from ego's generation and descending. Ascendingly, for paternal uncles and aunts twice removed.

Tsu 族: Sib; tribe. Modifying indicator for relationships from the fourth collateral line and beyond.

Piao 表: Outside; external. Indicator of descent from father's sister, mother's brother and mother's sister. Similarly extended to all relatives descended from those whose terms include either *ku* (father's sister), *chiu* (mother's brother) or *i* (mother's sister).

Nei 內: Inside; inner; wife. Indicator of descent from wife's brother, or from relatives comparable with him, e. g., his male sib-cousins.

Wai 外: Outside. Reciprocal modifier indicating mother's parents and daughter's children.

The above generalizations are based on the connotations of the modern standard terminology. They are abstracted from the whole range of the nomenclature, with every term taken into consideration. Yet, because of the multitude of possible combinations for every Chinese character, exceptions are inevitable. These exceptions, few and relatively insignificant, will be evident when the whole system is reviewed.

TERMINOLOGICAL COMPOSITION

In the building of terms, the terminology for the nuclear group of relations is taken as a structural basis, with the exception of parent-child and husband-wife terms, which are used as sex indicators.[23] All modifying elements indicating collateral relationship and descent are prefixed,[24] in succession, to the chosen basis, with the element expressing the nearest relationship nearest the basis and that expressing the farthest relationship furthermost, until the desired relationship is reached. All sex indicators are suffixed. If the generation category of the structural basis is not apparent, as in *chiu* and *i*, the sex indicators also function as generation indicators; here, too, they are always suffixed.

In choosing the structural basis for a term of a relationship, the factors to be considered are, first, generation and second, descent. Take, for example, the term for the father's father's sister's son's daughter's son. This is a complicated one, since the

---

[23] The sex indicators are *fu* 父, *mu* 母, *tzŭ* 子, *nü* 女, *fu* 夫, *fu* 婦, *hsi* 媳, *hsü* 壻. Failure to recognize this set of terms has resulted in much misunderstanding of the system. The first to dispell this misunderstanding was perhaps H. P. WILKINSON, Chinese Family Nomenclature, *New China Rev.* (1921) 159-191. He writes: "The initial error of the writers ... was ... in taking the sex indicators for male and female appended to varying 'descriptive' appellations of kindred as the name of a class,—that of 'sons' and 'daughters.'" A. L. KROEBER, quite independently, also discovered that "these last four terms (i.e. *fu* 父, *mu* 母, *fu* 夫, *fu* 婦) merely denote the sex of the person referred to, when they are added to other kinship terms. ..." Process in the Chinese Kinship System, *American Anthropologist* 35 (1933) 151-157.

[24] The terms "prefixing" and "suffixing" are employed here in a loose sense, since there are no true "prefixes" and "suffixes" in Chinese (with the exception, perhaps, of a few elements, notably the nominal suffixes). Here they merely indicate that a certain indivisible element (character) is placed *before* or *after* another indivisible element (character) in syntactic relationship.

descent has shifted from female to male, and then back to female. Disregarding descent, let us first consider the generation. The individual concerned is of the son's generation. Instantly the basis is reduced to the alternatives *chih* or *wai shêng*. His immediate relationship with ego is through a female relative of ego's generation; therefore, the term *chih* is eliminated and only *wai shêng* remains. Furthermore, his relationship is a non-sib but consanguineal one, and descent is from father's father's sister, a relationship comparable with father's sister's; therefore, the qualifying elements *ku* and *piao* should be added. He belongs to the third collateral line of non-sib reatives; therefore, the collateral modifier *t'ang* is applicable. Together, these elements form the term *t'ang ku piao wai shêng*—a term as exact as can be desired. To express a female relationship of the same kind, add *nü* to the above term, making it *t'ang ku piao wai shêng nü* [that is, f f si s d d]. To express a female relationship by marriage, substitute *fu* for *nü*; for a male relationship by marriage, substitute *hsü*.

The elements which make up a compound term should always be interpreted in their extended, that is, their secondary, meanings, and should never be understood in their primary meanings. The amalgamation of all the extended meanings makes up the new connotation of the term so compounded. This phenomenon is a feature of Chinese syntax. Failure to understand this has been the source of much misinterpretation.

The following illustrations represent practically the whole range of the structural bases. They are chosen with a view to including the widest variety of combinations, in order to elucidate the nature of terminological formations. The scope, however, is naturally limited, and fuller information must be sought in the tables.

Examples. The *italics* represent the nuclear term used as a structural basis, and the roman, the added modifiers:

tsu	f f	ku piao *po* fu	f f si s $>$ f
po *tsu* mu	f f o b w	*shu*	f y b
t'ang shu *tsu* fu	f f f b s $<$ f f	t'ang *shu* mu	w of f f b s $<$ f
po	f o b	tsai ts'ung *shu* fu	f f f b s s $<$ f
t'ang *po* fu	f f b s $>$ f	*ku*	f si

PRINCIPLES OF TERMINOLOGICAL COMPOSITION 13

t'ang *ku* fu	f f b d h		t'ang *tzŭ* fu	h of f b d ⟩ e
ku piao *ku* mu	f f si d		t'ang i piao *tzŭ* fu	h of m f b d d⟩e
chiu	m b		*mei*	y si
t'ang *chiu* fu	m f b s		i *mei*	w y si
t'ang piao *chiu* fu	m f f si s s		t'ang i *mei* fu	h of w f b d ⟨ w
i	m si		i piao *mei* fu	h of m si d ⟨ e
t'ang *i* fu	m f b d h		t'ang i piao *mei*	m f b d d ⟨ e
tsai ts'ung *i* mu	m f f b s d		*chih*	b s
hsiung	o b		tsu *chih* nü	f f f b s s s d
ku piao *hsiung*	f si s ⟩ e		tsai ts'ung *chih* hsü	f f b s s d h
t'ang ku piao *hsiung*	f f si s s ⟩ e		*wai shêng*	si s
sao	o b w		t'ang *wai shêng* nü	f b d d
chiu piao *sao*	w of m b s ⟩ e		t'ang ku piao *wai shêng*	f f si s d s
t'ang chiu piao *sao*	w of m f b s s ⟩ e		*sun*	s s
ti	y b		chih *sun* nü	b s d
t'ang *ti* fu	w of f b s ⟨ e		t'ang chih *sun*	f b s s s
tsai ts'ung *ti*	f f b s s ⟨ e		wai shêng *sun* hsü	si s d h
tzŭ	o si			

In building terms for the third and fourth ascending and descending generations, the terms of the second ascending and descending generations are used as a basis, generation indicators are added to them. Modifiers of descent are usually added first, before the generation modifiers are prefixed. Examples:

tsu	f f		*sun*	s s
tsêng *tsu* mu	f f m		tsêng *sun* nü	s s d
tsêng po *tsu* fu	f f f o b		tsêng chih *sun* fu	b s s s w
kao *tsu* fu	f f f f		hsüan *sun*	s s s s

The above represent the compositional principles of the standard system.[25] The standard terms are universal and form the patterns on which other terms are built or formed. They are for the most part used in formal—i. e., genealogical, legal and ceremonial—literature. In ordinary applications, they must be properly qualified by modifiers according to the specific situations under which they are used.

REFERENTIAL MODIFIERS

The referential modifiers actually reflect the Chinese social code of etiquette, as well as the Chinese psychology concerning the proper attitudes to be assumed in social intercourse. It is a sign

[25] Some would call it "literary system," in the broad sense of the term.

of politeness and refinement to pay due respect and compliments to others, and, appropriately but not exaggeratedly, to maintain for oneself a more or less humble position. This is precisely the attitude that conditions the application of kinship terms.

The referential modifiers are also a manifestation of the consciousness of membership in the relational group. The complimentary and depreciatory modifiers cannot be applied indiscriminately; their application is prescribed by the identification with one relational group in contrast with another. Compliments may be applied more loosely, but depreciatives can be used only to those whom one strictly considers members of one's own relational group.

These two attitudes are fundamental in the application and understanding of the whole terminology.

The referential modifiers are governed by definite rules concerning their applications, and are always prefixed to the standard terms. With respect to their nature and usages, all of them can be broadly grouped under the following categories: 1. Complimentary, 2. Depreciatory, 3. Self-reference, 4. Posthumous.

Complimentary. These elements are used in referring to the relatives of the person to whom one is speaking or writing. They consist of the following three elements: i. Ling 令: Illustrious, worthy, honorable. It may be prefixed to any standard term, except in instances where special stems are provided. ii. Tsun 尊: Honorable, venerable. Used synonymously with *ling*, but restricted in that it refers only to relatives of higher generation or status than that of the person to whom one is speaking. iii. Hsien 賢: Virtuous, worthy. Used alternatively with *ling*, but restricted in that it refers only to relatives of lower generation and status than that of the person to whom one is speaking. There are a few exceptions to this rule, e. g., *hsien shu*, " your virtuous paternal uncle."

Whenever one is in doubt as to whether *tsun* or *hsien* should be prefixed, he uses *ling*. *Ling, tsun* and *hsien* have the sense of " your " used in a polite way.

Complimentary modifiers should be prefixed when speaking to persons not related to oneself. They should not be used between sib relatives, except, when speaking to those of lower generations, in reference to their superiors. This latter practice is really teknonymy. The complimentary modifiers should be prefixed when reference is made to the relative of a non-sib relative to whom one is speaking, if that individual is not a connecting relative. If he is a connecting relative and of higher generation than the speaker, the usual standard or vocative kinship term should be used. As a rule, one does not compliment those with whom one has close and direct relationships.

Depreciatory.[26] These modifiers are prefixed to the standard terms in referring to one's own relatives of the same sibname, when speaking or writing to others. "Depreciatory" is used here in the sense of "modest" or "of one's own." They consist of the following three elements: i. Chia 家: Family, dwelling, household. It is prefixed to the terms of all sib relatives of higher generation and status than ego. ii. Shê 舍: Cottage, shed, household. It is prefixed to the terms of sib relatives of the generation of, but of lower status than, ego (as younger brother); and principally in reference to sib relatives of the first descending generation, and sometimes all descending generations. It should never be used in reference to relatives in the direct lineal line, e. g., for one's own children. iii. Hsiao 小: Minor, junior, small, diminutive. Prefixed to the terms of sib relatives of lower generation than that of ego, principally in reference to one's own children, grandchildren, etc. With the exception of the lineal descendants, *shê* and *hsiao* can be used synonymously.

Chia, *shê* and *hsiao* have somewhat the sense of "my" used in a modest manner. It is important to note that depreciatory modifiers are not applicable to relatives of a different sibname.[27] They are not even applicable to one's father's married sisters or one's own married sisters because these women have adopted their husband's sibnames and are no longer considered as members of

---

[26] "Depreciatory" is used in contrast to "Complimentary." As the elements *chia* and *shê* show, "depreciatory" is used in the sense of "of my own family" or "of my own sib."

[27] There is a general term that can be applied to any non-sib relative, i. e., *pi chʻin* 敝親. "my poor [or unworthy] relative."

one's own family or sib, and therefore they are not to be "depreciated."[28]

Self-reference.[29] These modifiers are prefixed to the terms used by ego to refer to himself before another relative, either in speaking or in writing, e. g., a nephew refers to himself before an uncle, or vice versa. They consist of the following two elements: i. Yü 愚: Simple, rude, stupid. It can be prefixed to the terms when used by ego to refer to himself, principally as a relative of higher generation to one of lower generation. ii. Hsiao 小: Junior, minor. It can be prefixed to the terms when used by ego to refer to himself, principally where a relative of lower generation address one of higher generation.

Neither *yü* nor *hsiao* are applicable to oneself where addressing a relative of the direct lineal line, e. g., father and son, grandfather and grandson, etc., where special terms are provided for such purposes.

Posthumous. These modifiers are prefixed to—excepting a few special stems for this purpose—the standard terms when used in reference to one's own dead relatives, especially for parents, grandparents, father's brothers, etc. They consist of the following two elements: i. Wang 亡: "Deceased." Prefixed to terms of all relatives when dead. ii. Hsien 先: "The late," "the former." Prefixed only to terms of relatives of higher generation or status than ego, when dead.

When referring to the dead relatives of others the complimentary modifiers must again be prefix to these modifiers. This practice is not common; usually a circumlocutory expression is employed.

There are a number of special stems which are used with the referential modifiers. They will be pointed out in the tables (see pp. 207-265) in each connection. For the sake of clarity and brevity, all terms qualified by the referential modifiers, or formed with

---

[28] *Yen shih chia hsün* 風操篇, 2.5a 凡言姑，姊，妹，女子子，已嫁則以夫氏稱之，在室則以次第稱之．言禮成他族，不得云家也．

[29] "Self-reference" modifiers are in a certain respect indistinguishable from "depreciatory" except in context. It is especially true of the element *hsiao*. They are separated here for the purpose of exposition.

Principles of Terminological Composition

special words, will be called in later discussion either complimentary, depreciatory, self-reference, or posthumous terminologies.

Vocative Terms

Vocatives are used as forms of addressing relatives direct in person. In literary address, i. e., in writing, the standard terms must be used. Vocatives must not be used together with referential modifiers. The latter can only be prefixed to standard terms.

Vocatives are limited to relatives of higher generations than ego, and to those of the same generation as, but of higher age status than, ego. Relatives of lower generations and age status can be addressed by name, or by using the standard terms as vocatives, if the occasion should arise. All vocatives are formed from three groups of terms: grandparent terms, parent terms, and older sibling terms.

Grandparent terms. The grandparent vocatives vary a great deal with local usage. As they have not been systematically recorded, it is rather difficult to determine the most prevalent ones. *Yeh yeh, wêng* or *wêng wêng, kung* or *kung kung,* for paternal grandfather, *p'o* or *p'o p'o, nai nai,* for paternal grandmother, may be considered the most common. No matter which terms are adopted in local usage, the adopted local terms are extended consistently throughout the whole system like these forms. In their extension, they are suffixed to the standard terminology by dropping the *tsu fu* and *tsu mu,* e. g., for *po tsu fu* (f f o b) the vocative is *po wêng,* or *po kung.*

Parent terms. Parent terms are less variable than grandparent terms. *Tieh, yeh,* and *pa pa* for father; *ma* and *niang* for mother. *Pa pa* is never, and *niang* is seldom, used in extensions.

Tieh 爹: Vocative for father. Used to form vocative terms for male relatives of the first ascending generation in place of *fu*.

Ma 媽: Vocative for mother. Used to form vocative terms for female relatives of the first ascending generation in place of *mu*.[30]

The above rules will not apply in instances where special

---

[30] *Ma* and *mu,* in their extensions, indicate a married status, and cannot be applied to unmarried female relatives.

vocatives are provided. These terms may also be omitted in certain cases where they are unnecessary, just as *fu* and *mu* are sometimes omitted.

Older sibling terms. Ko, or ko ko 哥哥: Vocative for older brother. Used for conjugating vocative terms in place of *hsiung* for male relatives of the generation of, but older than, ego.

Chieh, or chieh chieh 姐姐: Vocative for older sister. Used for conjugating vocative terms in place of *tzŭ* for female relatives of the generation of, but older than, ego.

It is the vocative nomenclature that varies dialectically. At present, this variability mostly involves the grandparent and parent terms, the older sibling terms showing very little variation. But no matter how variable the dialectical vocatives may be, the above conjugation rules can be applied simply by replacing the given forms with local terms.

The vocative terms are used more loosely, i. e., they are more "classificatory" than the standard terminology. When two relatives speak face to face the exact relationship is always understood; it is only in referential usages that the more exact terms are needed. The prevalent use of sibnames,[31] personal names, titles, and numerical order of seniority and juniority [32] for par-

---

[31] Sibnames are used only for particularizing non-sib relatives and women married into the sib.

[32] The ancient method of denoting seniority and juniority by *po* 伯, *chung* 仲, *shu* 叔, and *chi* 季 has long been obsolete. A purely numerical order is used today. If ego's father is one of six siblings, A, b, C, D, e, and F (capitals indicate males, small letters, females), the numerical order of *ta* 大, *êrh* 二, *san* 三, *ssŭ* 四, *wu* 五 and *liu* 六 will be applied to them, respectively. *Ta* is used in the sense of "eldest." Jih chih lu, 23. 38a: 今人兄弟行次，稱一爲大，不知始自何時。漢淮南厲王常謂上大兄，孝文帝行非第一也. If ego's father is D, then ego will call A *ta po*, b *êrh ku*, C *san po*, e *wu ku*, and F *liu shu*. If ego's father is A, then ego will call b *êrh ku*, C *san shu*, D *ssŭ shu*, e *wu ku*, and F *liu shu*. The terms *po* and *shu* change positions in accordance with the relative order of ego's father, but the numerical order remains constant.

There is another method of assigning the numerical order, viz., by separating the male and the female series. As in the above case, A, C, D, and F will be assigned *ta, êrh, san* and *ssŭ*, respectively, and b, e will be given *ta, êrh* respectively. The method used depends upon local custom and family whim.

ticularizing each relative in vocative address also makes the accurate system rather too cumbersome.

Supernumerary Terms

There are a few groups of terms which may be called "supernumerary,"[33] viz., the sacrificial, epitaphic, literary and alternative names. These are referred to in the tables on pp. 207-265.

Sacrificial terms were used in ancient times for the direct lineal ancestors when offering sacrifices to them. There are only a few such terms, but they are now obsolete. Epitaphic terms are used on epitaphs and monuments. Strictly speaking, there are only two such terms, k'ao 考 for father and pi 妣 for mother. It is only the sons who erect epitaphs for their parents. Sacrificial and epitaphic terms are often confused with terms modified by "posthumous" modifiers. They are frequently used interchangeably, since they all refer to dead relatives, although in slightly different senses. Nevertheless, there are some very interesting changes which are of historical significance.

Literary terms are those used only in literary compositions, usually non-vocative and non-referential. Many of them are old obsolete terms but still retained in literary usage. Alternative terms are those that can be used synonymously with the prevalent forms. The adoption of the one or the other depends entirely upon local custom and individual proclivities.

---

[33] "Supernumerary" is employed here in the sense used by E. W. Gifford in his discussion of *California Kinship Terminologies*, UC-PAAE 18, 1922-1926. It is not a happy term, and is adopted here only for want of a better one.

STRUCTURAL PRINCIPLES AND TERMINOLOGICAL CATEGORIES

The architectonic structure of the Chinese system is based upon two principles: lineal and collateral differentiation, and generation stratification. The former is a vertical, and the latter a horizontal, segmentation. Through the interlocking of these two principles, every relative is rigidly fixed in the structure of the whole system.

Lineal and Collateral Differentiation

The methods of differentiating collaterals differ in the ancient and the modern systems. In the ancient system, the *Êrh Ya* and *I Li*, each collateral line is differentiated by following the terminology of the kin nearest to the lineal line from whom this line originated; e. g., father's father's father's brother is called *tsu* tsêng wang fu, and his descendants down to ego's generations are differentiated by prefixing the term *tsu* to their respective terms; father's father's brother is called *ts'ung tsu* wang fu, and all his descendants down to ego's generation are differentiated by prefixing the term *ts'ung tsu*. This method is also applied to more remote collateral lines.[1]

In the *Êrh Ya* system there is no term for brother's sons and their descendants, nor is there any term for father's brother's son's sons and their descendants, nor for father's father's brother's son's son's sons and their descendants. It seems that the sons of brothers and sib-brothers merge into one another, i. e. brother's sons are one's own sons. On the other hand, the *Êrh Ya* gives the term *ch'u*[2] for sister's son (man speaking), *li sun*[3] for sister's son's son (man speaking); *chih*[4] for brother's son (woman speaking), *kuei sun*[5] for brother's son's son (woman speaking). In the strict patrilineal sib organization of the Chou period, even one's own sons are differentiated from one another as regards the order

---

[1] Cf. CHÊNG Chên: 補正爾雅釋親宗族, *Ch'ao ching ch'ao wên chi*, 1.1a-4b.
[2] *Êrh Ya*: 男子謂姊妹之子爲出.
[3] *Ibid.*: 謂出之子爲離孫.
[4] *Ibid.*: 女子謂昆弟之子爲姪.
[5] *Ibid.*: 謂姪之子爲歸孫.

of succession, hence it is difficult to see why there are no terms to differentiate one's own sons from brother's sons and sib-brother's sons, while, on the contrary, terms are provided whereby the man may differentiate his sons from his sister's sons, and the woman may differentiate her sons from her brother's sons.[6]

The differentiating of collaterals in the modern system is far more complete and consistent, but is carried out on a different principle. The generation stratum of ego is used as a basis, and the collateral modifying terminology is extended vertically downward and upward. E. g., father's brother's sons are called *t'ang hsiung ti*, their sons and grandsons are called *t'ang chih* and *t'ang chih sun*, respectively. Upwards, *t'ang* is extended to father's father's brother's son, e. g., *t'ang po fu* and *t'ang shu fu*; and to father's father's father's brother's sons, e. g., *t'ang po tsu fu* and *t'ang shu tsu fu*. Other collateral lines, e. g., *tsai-ts'ung* and *tsu*, are similarly extended.

The development of the modern principle of differentiation began in the Han period. First came the differentiation of one's own sons from brother's sons by employing the terms *yu tzŭ* or *ts'ung tzŭ*.[7] During the Chin period the term *chih* was permanently changed from a woman's term for brother's son to a man's term for brother's son. *T'ung t'ang*[8] was first used during the fifth and sixth centuries for denoting the second collateral line, and was later abbreviated to *t'ang*. *Tsai ts'ung* came into use a little later, and *tsu* is an old term used in a slightly delimited sense. With these important collateral modifying terminologies perfected, the whole process was completed about the end of the first millennium A. D.

[6] It is very doubtful whether the *Êrh Ya* system is complete. It also has no terms for f si s s, m b s s, and m si s s. By inference, f si s s and m b s s can be called *ch'u*, since sister's husband, f si s, and m b s are called *shêng*, and sister's son is called *ch'u*. But the absence of terms for m si s s is rather disconcerting; these terms cannot all be merged into the terms for ego's own sons, or into any others. For some reason or other the compilers of the *Êrh Ya* seem not to have been interested in the terms for descendants of collaterals of the same generation. On the other hand, the *Êrh Ya* system, as it stands, seems to stress the terms on the matrilineal side of descending generations. Whether or not this is a survival of an earlier matrilineate is a matter of interpretation, since other evidence is inconclusive.

[7] Cf. Table I, No. 125. [8] Cf. Table I, No. 41.

DIAGRAM I
Ancient System of Collateral Differentiation

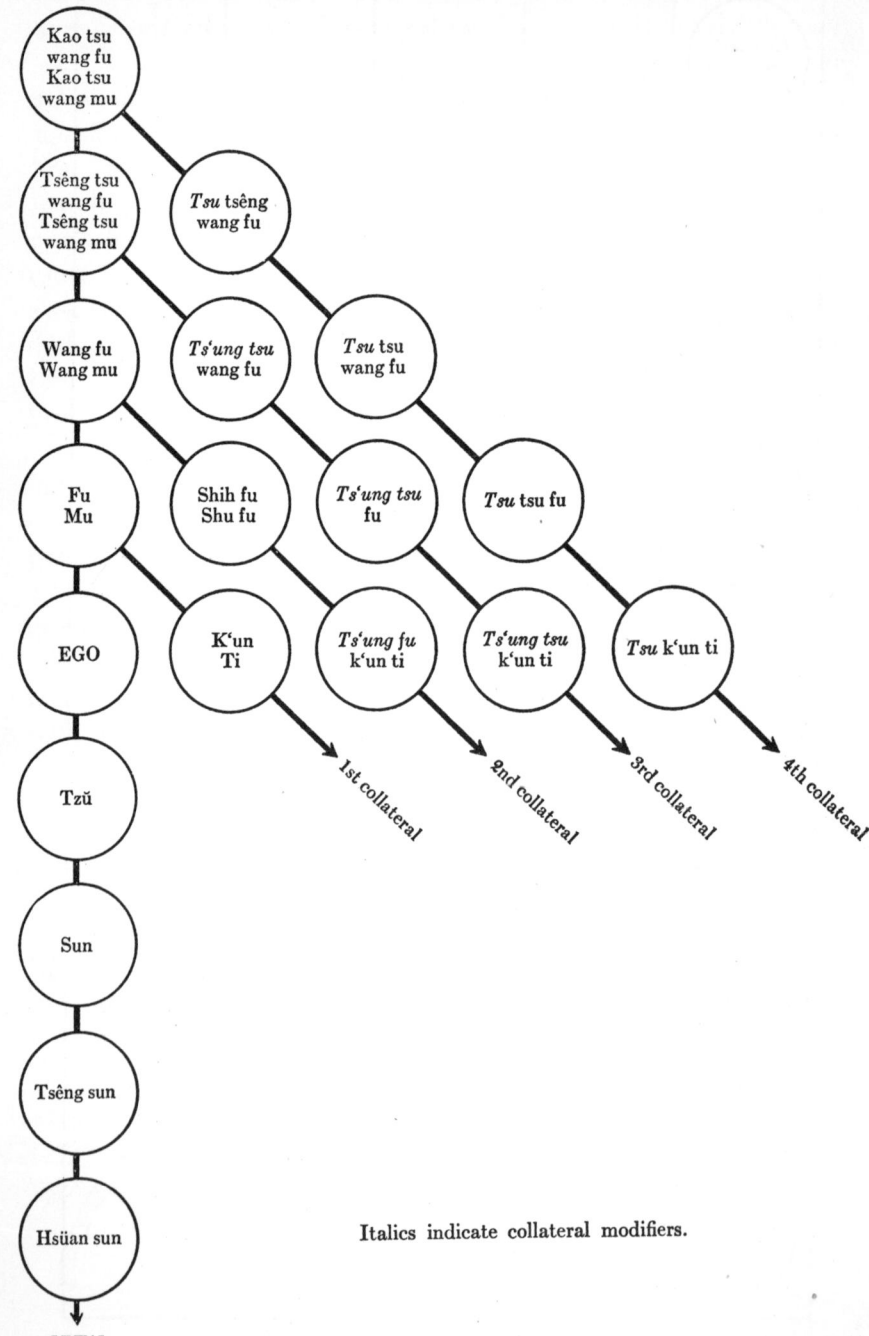

Italics indicate collateral modifiers.

STRUCTURAL PRINCIPLES AND TERMINOLOGICAL CATEGORIES 23

Diagram II
Modern System of Collateral Differentiation

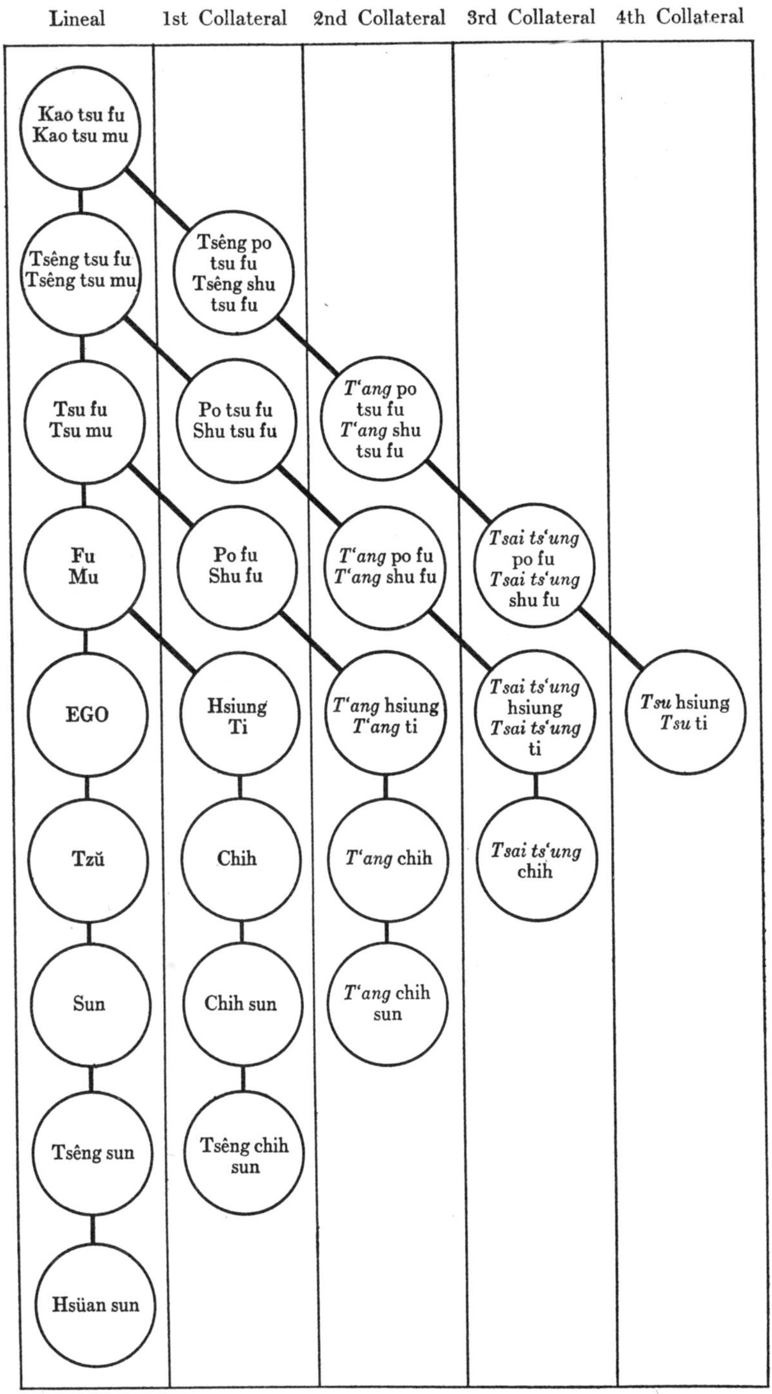

Lineal	1st Collateral	2nd Collateral	3rd Collateral	4th Collateral
Kao tsu fu / Kao tsu mu				
Tsêng tsu fu / Tsêng tsu mu	Tsêng po tsu fu / Tsêng shu tsu fu			
Tsu fu / Tsu mu	Po tsu fu / Shu tsu fu	T'ang po tsu fu / T'ang shu tsu fu		
Fu / Mu	Po fu / Shu fu	T'ang po fu / T'ang shu fu	Tsai ts'ung po fu / Tsai ts'ung shu fu	
EGO	Hsiung / Ti	T'ang hsiung / T'ang ti	Tsai ts'ung hsiung / Tsai ts'ung ti	Tsu hsiung / Tsu ti
Tzǔ	Chih	T'ang chih	Tsai ts'ung chih	
Sun	Chih sun	T'ang chih sun		
Tsêng sun	Tsêng chih sun			
Hsüan sun				

Italics indicate collateral modifiers.

Generation Stratification

All relatives in the system are stratified in successive generation layers. This stratification performs the important function of fixing the exact location of relatives in the system, in conjunction with the principle of collateral differentiation.

In diagram III (see p. 166), the vertical columns represent collaterals and the horizontal columns represent generations. When one set of columns is superimposed upon the other, the two afford pigeonholes for every relative in the system. Each relative is then rigidly fixed, and not subject to fluctuations. The generation strata are maintained by the use of *generation* modifiers. The modifiers are, in most cases, adapted from the nuclear terms from the direct lineal line, since in counting generations the lineal relatives are always used as absolute standards of measure. This adaptation of nuclear kinship terms as generation indicators has been interpreted as partial merging of collaterals and lineals. Given our present knowledge of the system, this interpretation is not tenable.

Since generation is an important structural principle, it must not be disrupted, lest the structure break down. The most serious, if not the only, disruptive factor in this principle is intergeneration marriage. To counteract this influence, generation has become an important factor in the regulation of marital relations. A Chinese is not required to marry any of his or her relatives, but if such marriages do occur between relatives both parties must belong to the same generation stratum. In other words, a Chinese may marry any person outside of his or her own sib; if the parties are related, they must be of the same generation, irrespective of age.

This rule seems to have been less stringent in ancient times. During the Chou period a feudal lord could take his wife's paternal nieces as concubines, or even as wives after his wife's death. The Han emperor, Hui Ti (194-188 B. C.), married his older sister's daughter,[9] and the T'ang emperor, Chung-tsung (705-710 A. D.),

---

[9] *Han shu* 外戚列傳, 97A 5a: [孝惠張皇后] 宣平侯敖尙帝姊魯元公主，有女，惠帝卽位，呂太后欲爲重親，以公主女配后爲皇后・・・

married his paternal grandaunt's daughter.[10] These instances are severely condemned as incestuous by later historians and moralists,[11] but they were not so condemned by contemporaries. On the other hand, these instances may have been anomalous; it may be only because the marriages involved emperors that they went unpunished and uncriticized. But, in either case, they do show the laxity of the generation rule during the earlier period.[12]

There can be no doubt that the generation rule was much stressed even during the Chou period,[13] since the recorded marriages show that the inter-generation type of marriage was the exception rather than the rule.[14] Its stiffening was gradual, and culminated about the middle of the first millennium A. D. The period of intensive development of the principle seems to have been about the third and fourth centuries A. D., because it is during this period that the generation indicators in personal names became popular. The T'ang Code (ca. 600 A. D.) contains clauses which definitely prohibit marriage between relatives of different generations.[15] All subsequent codes contain such interdictions, and cite cases. From the end of the first millennium A. D.

---

[10] *T'ang shu* 76. 19b: 中宗和思順聖皇后趙 ··· 父環, 尙高祖常樂公主, 帝爲英王, 聘后爲妃.

[11] WANG Ming-shêng (1723-1797 A. D.) discussed these instances in his 十七史商榷 (廣雅書局本) 86. 2a: as the most flagrant violations of the " relationships of humanity," 人倫之極變.

[12] The *T'ung tien* discussed two instances of difficulties in mourning obligations arising from inter-generation marriages, 95. 12a: 族父是姨弟爲服議; and the hypothetical case, 95. 5b-6b: 娶同堂姊之女爲妻, 姊亡服議. It seems that inter-generation marriage between distant relatives was tolerated during the first half of the first millennium A. D.

[13] Both the *tsung fa* and the *sang fu* institutions, which were developed during this period, stress the separation of generations. *Sang fu* will be dealt with later. As to *tsung fa*, the subdivisions of *tsung* into minor *tsung* 小宗, for the most part, depends upon the counting of generations.

[14] The instances of primary inter-generation marriages can be counted on the fingers. LIANG Yü-shêng [*P'ieh chi*, 2. 2a] says: 楚成王取文芊二女, (左僖廿二), 晉文公納嬴氏 (僖廿四), 皆以甥爲妻者, 可謂無別矣. 嗣後妻甥者, 漢孝惠取張敖女, 章帝取竇勳女, 吳孫休取朱據女, 俱楚顏晉重作之俑也.

[15] *T'ang lü shu* I 戶婚, 14. 2a: 若外姻有服屬, 而尊卑共爲婚姻 ··· 以姦論. This is followed by expositions of this clause, and by another clause of the same nature but more specific. 尊卑 means " relatives belonging to different generations."

Diagram III

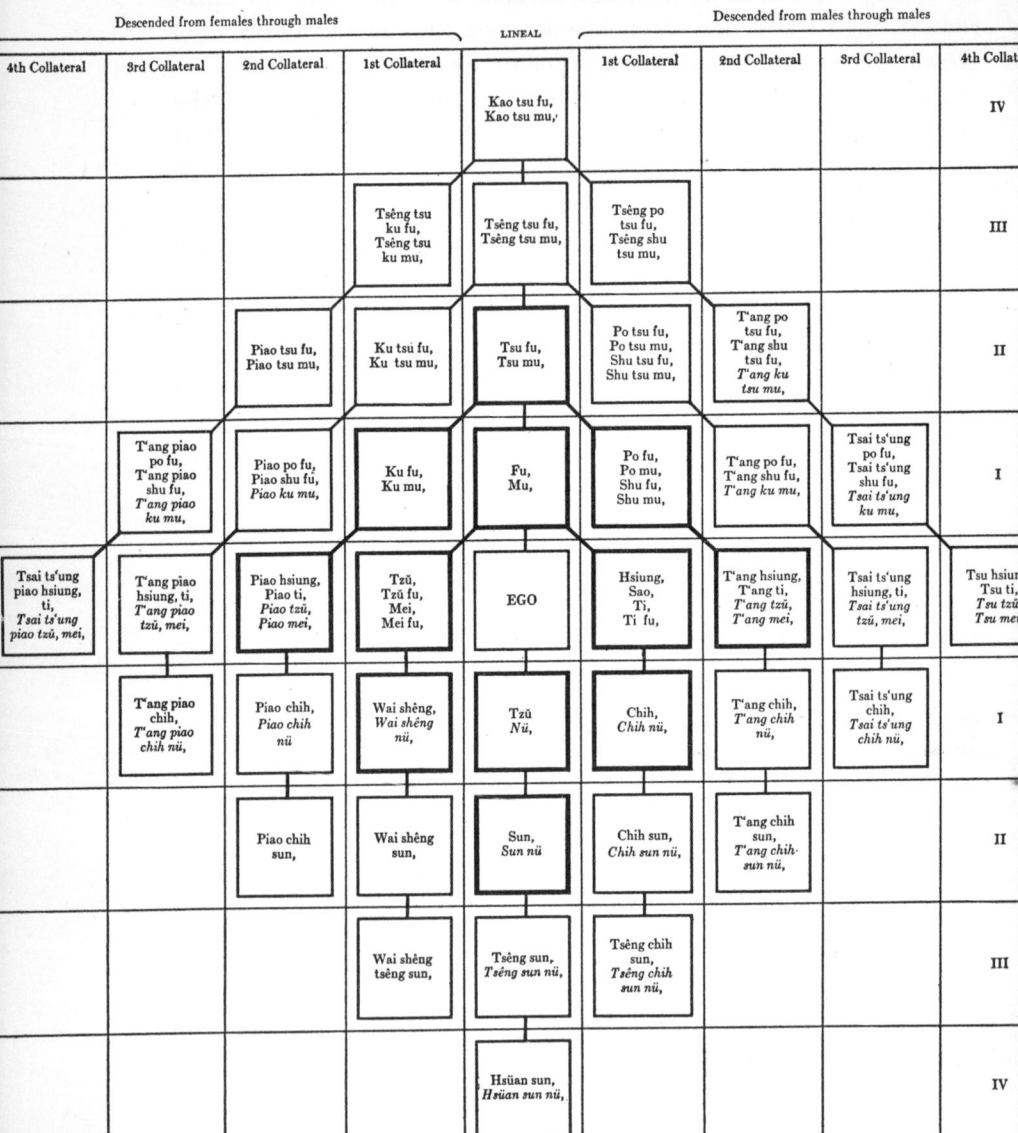

The heavy squares represent the nuclear group of relatives. Those in italics, indicate their descendants have not been carried over into the next generation, e. g., the children of *nü* are *wai sun* and *wai sun nü* but not given in the following square. The Roman numerals represent ascending and descending generations.

to the present, not only have inter-generation marriages been rigorously forbidden by law, but popular sentiment against them runs so high that even a teacher marrying his or her pupil, or a person marrying a friend's daughter or son, is condemned.

The underlying concept is the desire to keep constant the generation layers of relatives and to prevent their disruption. If the generation of one relative is disrupted by marriage, then all the positions of the relatives connected with him would also be disrupted, and the system would lose its accuracy of description and thus defeat its own purpose.

Categories

Kroeber's essay on the *Classificatory Systems of Relationship* [16] does not invalidate the use of classificatory and descriptive designations in anthropological discussion; its contribution lies in the establishment of categories that are inherent in all systems. These categories constitute a convenient means for examining the working processes of any system. It is impossible to tabulate the whole Chinese system into one table, but we may take the nuclear terms and tabulate them in the light of the eight categories suggested by Kroeber. It must be understood that these nuclear terms are also used in secondary meanings, qualified by modifiers. In this tabulation (see p. 168) only their primary meanings are considered.

Now let us consider the system as a whole, together with the nuclear terms under each category.

---

[16] *Journal, Royal Anthropological Institute of Great Britain and Ireland* 39 (1909). 77-84.

28 THE CHINESE KINSHIP SYSTEM

Categories	祖 tsu	孫 sun	父 fu	子 tzǔ	母 mu	女 nü	兄 hsiung	弟 ti	姊 tzǔ	妹 mei	伯 po	叔 shu	姪 chih	甥 shêng	舅 ku	舅 chiu	姨 i	岳 yo	婿 hsü	夫 fu	妻 ch'i	嫂 sao	婦 fu	Total	Percentage
Generation	*	*	*	*	*	*	*	*	*	*	*	*	*	*					*	*	*	*	*	18	78.27
Blood or marriage	*	*	*	*	*	*	*	*	*	*	*	*	*	*				*	*	*	*	*	*	18	78.27
Lineal or collateral	*	*	*	*	*	*	*	*	*	*	*	*	*	*	*	*	*	*	*	*	*	*	*	23	100
Sex of relative	*	*	*	*	*	*	*	*	*	*	*	*	*	*	*	*	*	*	*	*	*	*	*	23	100
Sex of connecting relative	*	*									*	*		*	*	*	*	*	*			*	*	13	56.53
Sex of speaker																								0	0
Age in generation							*	*	*	*	*	*										*	*	8	34.78
Condition of connecting relative																								0	0

NUCLEAR RELATIONSHIP TERMS CLASSIFIED ACCORDING TO KROEBER'S CATEGORIES

i. *The difference between persons of the same and of separate generations.* This category is rigorously observed in the whole system through the use of generation indicators. Generation is not only an important structural principle in the system but is also an important regulator of marriage and a determinator in the application of vocatives. But in the nuclear terminology it is represented by only 78.3 per cent. of the terms. In the terms po, shu, ku, chiu, i the generation category is overridden. This merging of generations is not inherent in the system, but has been produced through the disruptive force of teknonymy, which will be discussed later.

ii. *The difference between lineal and collateral relationships.* This category is strictly fixed in the whole system. Collateral lines are differentiated by special modifiers. Practically all the basic modifiers exist solely for the function of developing this category. In the nuclear nomenclature it is represented by 100 per cent of the terms.

iii. *The difference of age within one generation.* This category is only partially represented in the system. It is fully represented in ego's own generation, whether male or female. Among the ascending generations it is operative only among the male relatives, with the exception of the wives of male relatives. Among the descending generations it is not operative at all. In the nuclear terminology it is represented by only 34.8 per cent.

W. H. R. Rivers attributed the differentiation of age within one generation to the practice of tribal initiation, i. e., older brothers will be initiated before younger brothers.[17] Whether or not this be correct, it is the only general explanation seriously advanced. In ancient China there are vestiges of initiation rites, especially as recorded in the *I Li*[18] and *Li Chi*.[19] Whether or not these ancient initiation rites have anything to do with the expression of this category is by no means certain. Chinese authors usually connect it with the sib organization, *tsung fa*, since in this organization the older brothers have absolute priority over the younger brothers in the transmission of office and property, and special privileges in the sacrificial rites to ancestors and in carrying on the line in general.[20]

iv. *The sex of the relative.* This category is consistently carried out in the whole system through the employment of sex indicators. In the nuclear terminology the representation is 100 per cent.

v. *The sex of the speaker.* This category is entirely inoperative. The sex of the speaker is always understood but never expressed. But there are traces of this category in the ancient system. E. g., in the *Êrh Ya* and the *I Li*, the term *chih* is exclusively used as a woman's term for brother's children. A few other terms may have been used only as women's or men's terms, but here we are less certain.

vi. *The sex of the person through whom the relationship exists.* This category is fully expressed in the system through the use of special modifiers. E. g., *piao hsiung ti* may mean father's sister's sons, mother's brother's sons, or mother's sister's sons. But if we say *ku piao hsiung ti, chiu piao hsiung ti* and *i piao hsiung ti*, the terms are

---

[17] W. H. R. RIVERS, *Social Organization*, ed. by W. J. Perry, 1924, p. 189.
[18] 士冠禮.
[19] 冠義.
[20] CH'ÊNG Yao-t'ien 程瑤田 (1725-1814): *Tsung fa hsiao chi* 宗法小記 1.1a: 宗之道，兄道也． 大夫士之家，以兄統弟，而以弟事兄之道也． Ibid. 1. 1b: 尊祖故敬宗，宗之者，兄之也． 故曰：宗之道，兄道也．

exact, and refer to father's sister's sons, mother's brother's sons and mother's sister's sons, respectively. There are lapses in the vocative usages, since the exact status of the connecting relative is always understood and never expressed.

vii. *The distinction of blood relatives from connection by marriage.* With the exception of the terms *chiu* and *i*, this category is consistently expressed. The merging of mother's brother (consanguineal) and wife's brother (affinal) into *chiu*, and of mother's sister (consanguineal) and wife's sister (affineal) into *i*, is due to the influence of teknonymy. In the vocative usages the terminology is looser, because of the mutual adoption of each other's terms by husband and wife.

viii. *The condition of life of the person through whom relationship exists.* This category is present, but usually is not consistently expressed. The most common distinction is between the dead and living relatives, by the application of special modifiers. There are a few distinct terms for this purpose for parents, grandparents, paternal uncles, etc. Other conditions of life of the relative are not expressed, or are indicated only by circumlocutory expressions.

Certain of these categories (ii, iv, vi and possibly vii) are essential to the maintenance of a strict unilateral—patrilineal in Chinese—descent. It is also exactly these categories that find their fullest expression in the Chinese system. The great nicety in the distinction of dead and living ancestors (category viii) in the ancient terminology may have been due to ancestor worship, which is less prevalent now.

Reciprocity

In kinship systems there is usually the factor of reciprocity to influence the expression of certain categories. Reciprocity is of three kinds: logical or conceptual reciprocity, verbal reciprocity, and self-reciprocity, i. e., both conceptual and verbal.[21] It is not, on the whole, a feature of the modern Chinese system, since, to a certain extent, it is incompatible with the consistent expression of certain categories and exactitude in the discrimination of relatives.

In the ancient system there are traces of conceptual reciprocity. The *I Li*[22] says, " They call me *ku*, I call them *chih.*" Inversely it is also true: " They call me *chih*, I call them *ku.*" *Ku*, as used in the *Êrh Ya* and the *I Li*, means father's sister, and *chih* means brother's child (woman speaking), both male and female. In other words, *ku* " indicates the sex of the relative but not of the speaker," whereas *chih* " does not recognize the sex of the

[21] Cf. the definition of reciprocity suggested by A. L. KROEBER, *California Kinship Systems*, UC: PAAE 12, 9. 340, note 1; Zuni Kin and Clan, Anthropological Papers, *AMNH* 18 (1919). 78-81.

[22] 喪服 32. 1b: 傳曰：姪者，何也？謂吾姑者，吾謂之姪。

relative indicated, but does imply the sex of the speaker." [23] Therefore, *ku* and *chih* each involve a category which the other does not express. *Ku* and *chih* in their ancient usages are true conceptual reciprocals.

The *Êrh Ya* also states, " They call me *chiu*, I call them *shêng*." [24] *Chiu* is here used in the sense of mother's brother, and *shêng*, sister's child. But the reverse does not hold true. Actually this statement contradicts the other terms recorded in the *Êrh Ya* itself, since *shêng* was used in the sense of father's sister's son, mother's brother's son, sister's husband (man speaking), and wife's brother. The *Êrh Ya* also gives another term, *chu*, for the same relative, sister's child. It is very likely that the above statement is a later interpolation, since *chiu-shêng* was probably reciprocal from the Han to the T'ang periods.[25] The whole problem is complicated by the question of cross-cousin marriage and teknonymy, which will be dealt with later. In short, *chiu-shêng* could not have been reciprocal in the ancient system, but *shêng* was itself partially reciprocal, i. e., in the male sex only.[26]

These are the only traces of reciprocity that can be detected in the ancient system. The tendency toward the consistent use of categories later became so strong that even these few vestiges of ancient reciprocal terms have entirely disappeared from the modern system.

---

[23] A. L. KROEBER: *Classificatory System of Relationship* 81.

[24] This statement also occurs in the *I Li*, 喪服 33.9a: 傳曰：甥者，何也？謂吾舅者，吾謂之甥。

[25] During this period *chiu* was used for mother's brother alone, and *shêng* dropped all its other connotations and became simply a term for sister's child, e. g., *wai-shêng*.

[26] That is, *shêng* is used reciprocally between mother's brother's son, father's sister's son, sister's husband (M. S.), wife's brother, and male ego. They call male ego *shêng*, and male ego also calls them *shêng*.

FACTORS AFFECTING THE SYSTEM

In the course of development from the ancient to the modern system there has been a slow but persistent tendency toward systematization and more exactly descriptive efficacy in nomenclature. This tendency has to a large extent been conditioned by the sociological lines along which Chinese society is organized, and has to a lesser extent been intentionally fostered by ardent ritualists and framers of etiquette. On the other hand, there are also potent social forces which work against overrationalization and oftentimes throw certain parts of the system out of gear by undermining certain categories. The systematizing forces are the sib-organization and the mourning system. These two factors have supplemented one another in moulding the kinship system to their own pattern. The disrupting forces are the Chinese marriage customs and, most potent of all, teknonymy. The ritualists served as a stabilizing agency in vigilantly conserving the nomenclature,[1] with a view to the exactitude of mourning specifications and the needs for maintaining sib solidarity. But generally they were powerless against the popular tendencies in kinship usages, and very often were forced to accept the already established terms and attempt to harmonize and incorporate them into the whole system.[2] Thus, in the Chinese system there is a seeming embodiment of a well considered plan while, at the same time, there are many incongruities. No matter how much we may discredit " mock kinship algebra," to borrow a phrase from Malinowski,[3] it is pertinent to inquire into the conflicting forces which have moulded, and are today shaping, the Chinese system.

---

[1] For example, *chiu* and *ku* as terms for the husband's parents have been obsolete since the turn of the first millennium A. D., but they are still used in this sense in ritual works. *Chiu* was extended to include wife's brother ca. 900 A. D., but one never finds *chiu* used in this sense in formal literature.

[2] E. g., *i* was extended to include mother's sister ca. 500 B. C. During the next seven or eight centuries, the new and old terms were used interchangeably. About 400 A. D. *i* was standardized as a term for both mother's sister and wife's sister.

[3] Kinship, *Man* 30 (1930). 17. 19-29.

The Sib: Descent and Exogamy

Kinship ties necessarily begin within the family as a procreational unit. These primary ties, as we may call them,[4] are biologically the same in all societies,[5] though, functionally, they may differ from culture to culture.[6] But kinship ties do not rest within the reproductive family. They are extended to a much wider circle of individuals who are actually or reputedly related to those of the procreational family. In this process of extension certain groups of related individuals are emphasized and certain others minimized, although their degree of relationship may be exactly the same. The basis of this variability in the grouping of kin is the subject of much, perhaps unduly much, anthropological discussion. And naturally so, for it is precisely this variability in kinship patterning that differs so widely among different peoples—particular systems grouping relatives in quite different ways. The character of the kin groups emphasized likewise reflects the wider ranges of the social structure of which the kinship system is part.

In the Chinese kinship system, relatives in the male line receive emphasis; the formalized basis of which is the exogamous patrilineal sib.

Sib organization is called *tsung fa* in Chinese, literally, the "law of kindred." The *tsung fa* was bound up with the feudal system,[7] which was swept away in the course of the third century B. C. The sib organization, however, has survived to the present day, although in a much attenuated and modified form. The postfeudal development of the sib reached its climax in the third to the eighth centuries A. D., when it is usually termed *shih tsu* or

---

[4] B. MALINOWSKI would call this "the initial situation of kinship": preface to Raymond FIRTH's *We, The Tikopia* [1936] x.

[5] I. e., the divisions into father, mother, son, daughter, brother and sister, members of the strictly procreational family, exist in all kinship systems.

[6] E. g., the relationship of "father" to the rest of the procreational group in a patrilineal society may be radically different from that in a matrilineal society.

[7] For the sib organization of the feudal period, cf. WAN Kuang-t'ai 萬光泰, *Tsung fa piao* 宗法表; WAN Ssŭ-ta 萬斯大, *Tsung fa lun* 宗法論; and CH'ÊNG Yao-t'ien 程瑤田, *Tsung fa hsiao chi* 宗法小記. For a more modern study, cf. SUN Yao 孫曜, *Ch'un ch'iu shih tai chih shih tsu* 春秋時代之世族 [1931].

tsung tsu. The causes of this excessive development were many, but primarily it represents a reactionary growth following the abolition of the feudal system. The larger and more prominent sibs took the place of the feudal nobility, both in monopolizing governmental offices and in maintaining social prestige.[8] Their influence began to decline during the T'ang period. This was, on the one hand, due to the suppressive measures of the T'ang rulers and, on the other hand, to the social upheavals precipitated by the decline of the T'ang dynasty.[9] At the present time sib organization, for most people, is less vital than formerly, but its traditions and influences still permeate the whole of Chinese social life.

Tsung fa itself has been well studied, and we need here consider only those two of its characteristics which have direct influence upon the alignment of relatives, viz., patrilineal descent and exogamy. With the *tsung*, the sib, each line of descent is strictly patrilineal, not only in the transmission of the sibname but also in the transmission of office, property, etc. It is also primogenitary: the eldest brother has priority over the younger brothers.[10] The *tsung* is absolutely exogamous. Marriage within it is impossible, even after a "hundred generations." It is also strictly patrilocal.[11] Evidence is far from conclusive as to whether or not Chinese society passed through a prior matrilineal phase.[12] Exogamy, however, was predominately a Chou institution,[13] and

[8] Cf. *Kai yü ts'ung k'ao*, 六朝重世族, 17. 1b-9a.

[9] Cf. *T'ung Chih* 通志：氏族略序, 25. 1.

[10] In the transmission of hereditary titles, the primogenitary principle holds but the property is divided equally among the brothers, although the eldest brother usually receives an extra share. It is only in the ceremonies in the ancestral halls that the primogenitary line has absolute priority over all collateral lines.

[11] When, for want of male issue, a son-in-law is adopted as son, he adopts the wife's sibname and lives with her parents. He is in every way treated as a son. The children of the third generation revert to his original sibname 三代回宗, but usually one male child is allowed to carry on the wife's line.

[12] The existence of an early matrilineal state constitutes the underlying hypothesis of many recent works on ancient Chinese society, e. g., M. GRANET's *La civilisation chinoise*, Paris, 1929, and Kuo Mo-jo's 中國古代社會研究, 1931. The evidence they have marshalled is suggestive rather than conclusive.

[13] *Li Chi* 大傳, 34. 7b: 繫之以姓而弗別，綴之以食而弗殊，雖百世而昏姻不通者，周道然也。 *T'ung Tien*, 96. 2a, cites 晉范汪祭典：且同姓百代不婚，周道也。

its development was rather late. Ancient authorities attest that during the Hsia and Shang [ca. 1700-1100 B. C.] periods members of the same sib could marry after the lapse of five generations.[14] The institution of strict sib exogamy was traditionally attributed to Chou Kung [ca. 1100 B. C.], who instituted it for the maintenance of sib solidarity. Nevertheless, there is abundant evidence to show that even during the Chou period this interdiction was neither universal nor strictly enforced.[15] It was only after the overthrow of the feudal system and the transformation of the sib organization that absolute sib exogamy gradually prevailed. From the middle of the first millennium A. D. to the present this rule has been vigorously enforced by law.[16]

The moulding effect of the exogamous patrilineal sib is seen in the dichotomy of relatives in the system. Relatives are divided, along sib lines, into *sib relatives* [tsung ch'in] and *non-sib relatives* [wai ch'in or nei ch'in]. All sib relatives belong to the same sib of ego and possess the same sibname. Paternal relatives descended from females through males or females are non-sib relatives. Maternal and affinal relatives all belong to the non-sib group.

To maintain this distinction between the sib and non-sib groups, the terminology must be bifurcated in such a way that the paternal relatives descended from males through males are differentiated from those descended from females through males. This is carried out by differentiating the father's brother's sons [*t'ang hsiung ti*] and their descendants from father's sister's sons [*piao hsiung ti*] and their descendants; brother's sons [*chih*] from sister's sons [*wai shêng*]; son's sons [*sun*] from daughter's sons [*wai sun*]; and so on, ascendingly, descendingly, and collaterally. This bifurcation is necessary, since father's sister, sister, daughter, or any female sib relative who through sib exogamy has married into

---

[14] *T'ai p'ing yü lan* 太平御覽 [1808] 鮑氏 ed., 540. 7b-8a, cites 禮外傳. The five generations include the generation of ego. Even then, it is still very doubtful whether the Hsia and Yin peoples had any exogamy at all.

[15] CHAO I says [*Kai yu ts'ung k'ao*, 31. 2b-3a], 同姓爲婚, 莫如春秋時最多 and cites many cases to support his thesis. He concludes, 此皆春秋時亂俗也, 漢以後此事漸少.

[16] E. g., in *T'ang lü shu i* 14. 1a: 諸同姓爲婚者, 各徒二年, 總麻以上以姦論. Cf. Pierre HOANG: *Le mariage chinois au point de vue légal*, [1898] 43-53.

other sibs, and their descendants, belong, on account of patrilineal descent, to different sibs from ego.

Nevertheless, the emphasis upon the sib relatives is not so manifest in the whole kinship system as it might be. A partial explanation lies in the minute differentiation in the terminology, which to a certain extent has obscured this grouping. If we look at the application of the depreciatory modifiers, however, this emphasis at once becomes apparent. Only sib relatives are to be depreciated, inasmuch as they are regarded as members of one's own group. Non-sib relatives are not to be depreciated, since they are felt to be outside of one's own group.

Conceptually, sib relatives are considered nearer than non-sib relatives, even though their degree of remoteness from ego may be exactly the same. This is best expressed in the mourning obligations. The mourning period for paternal grandparents is one year, but for maternal grandparents only five months; for paternal uncle one year, and for maternal uncle five months; for father's brother's son nine months, and for mother's brother's son only three months. More instructive is the difference in mourning periods for a female sib relative before and after her marriage. The mourning period for father's unmarried sister, ego's unmarried sister, unmarried daughter, and brother's unmarried daughter, is one year; after their marriage, the mourning period is decreased to nine months, i. e., it is lessened by one degree. Therefore, we see that as long as these females remain unmarried they belong to ego's sib, but after marriage they belong to their husband's sibs. This transference through marriage has lessened their bond with the sib and, consequently, with ego.[17]

The nomenclature of the non-sib relatives is perhaps more expressive of this dual division of relatives. The differentiation between paternal grandparents [*tsu*] and maternal grandparents [*wai tsu*], paternal uncle [*po* and *shu*] and maternal uncle [*chiu*], paternal aunt [*ku*] and maternal aunt [*i*], is, of course, a regular

---

[17] The mourning obligations of an unmarried female to her paternal relatives are just the same as those of her brother. After marriage, all these obligations are lessened by one degree, and, reciprocally, obligations of these relatives to her are also lessened by one degree.

feature of a system based upon exogamous social grouping. But the interesting phenomenon is the merging of the father's sister's, mother's sister's, and mother's brother's descendants in the single term, *piao*.[18] *Piao*, as a term in itself, means "outside" or "external." The descendants of father's sister, and of mother's sister and brother, although consanguineal relatives of distinct affiliation, are all non-sib relatives, and hence their merging in the term *piao* is understandable.

The introduction and development of *piao* is also of historical interest. In the ancient system of the *Êrh Ya* and the *I Li*, father's sister's sons and mother's brother's sons were merged in the term *shêng*, through cross-cousin marriage.[19] Mother's sister's children, being parallel cousins, stood alone as *ts'ung mu hsiung ti* [for males] and *ts'ung mu tzŭ mei* [for females]. During the first two centuries A. D., with cross-cousin marriage already long in abeyance, father's sister's sons were designated as *wai* [outside], e. g., *wai hsiung ti*,[20] and mother's brother's sons as *nei* [inside], e. g., *nei hsiung ti*.[21] At about the same time [22] *chung* and *piao* were used as equivalents of *nei* and *wai*, since *chung* means "middle," "inside," and *piao* means "outside," "external."

During the last few centuries of the first millennium B. C. and the first few centuries A. D., mother's sister's sons were usually designated by the newly extended term *i*, e. g., *i hsiung ti*, although *ts'ung mu hsiung ti* was still permissible.

From the fourth to the seventh centuries A. D. constant confusion was produced through the use of the terms *nei* or *wai* for mother's sister's children, and, consequently, a confusion of relatives involving father's sister's, mother's brother's and mother's sister's descendants.[23] The reason for this may lie in the fact

---

[18] The *ku piao*, *chiu piao* and *i piao* are the three first-degree *piao* relationships of the Chinese system.

[19] See discussion under CROSS-COUSIN MARRIAGE, below, pp. 183-186.

[20] *I Li* 喪服, 33.9b: 姑之子. 鄭注: 外兄弟也.

[21] *Ibid.*, 33.10b: 舅之子. 鄭注: 內兄弟也.

[22] *Hou-Han shu* 鄭太傳, 100.2a-3a: ••• 公業懼,乃詭詞更對曰: ••• 又明公將帥,皆中表腹心.

[23] E. g., *T'ung Tien*, 95.9a-12b: 爲內外妹爲兄弟妻服議: (The instance involved is neither mother's brother's daughter, nor father's sister's daughter, who ought to be

that these relatives, although of clear affiliation, all belong to the non-sib group and are distinct from the exogamous partilineal sib group. During the Tʻang period, the *chung* was dropped and *piao* alone was applied to all these relatives.[24] Thus *piao* became a general indicator for non-sib consanguineal relations descended from relatives of higher generations than ego.

This conceptual as well as nomenclative dichotomy of relatives is a definitive expression of the exogamous patrilineal sib principle. At the same time, this principle has been modified by another factor—mourning rituals—resulting in the elaborate differentiation of collateral lines in the sib group, rather undermining its original function. But an understanding of this principle is most essential for a grasp of the system as a whole, since it is not only a potent moulding force but is as well a controlling factor in many important kinship usages, i. e., the depreciatory and complimentary terminologies.

Mourning Grades

The Chinese mourning system is based upon the sib organization for its discrimination against non-sib relatives, and on degree of relationships for the assignment of mourning grades. Mourning for sib relatives vanishes at the fourth degree [fourth collateral] and at the fourth generation, both ascending and descending from ego.[25] There is, consequently, in the kinship system a sharp differentiation of the first four collateral lines, and an indefinite grouping of all further collaterals in the *tsu* relationship.

Mourning, *sang fu* in Chinese, is a colossal subject in itself;

---

nei or *wai*, respectively, but mother's sister's daughter) 晉徐衆論云：徐恩龍娶姨妹爲婦，婦亡，而諸弟以姨妹爲嫂，嫂叔無服，不復爲姨妹行喪。 The 海錄碎事 (cited by *Chʻêng wei lu*, 3. 20a) states: 唐人兩姨之子，相謂爲外兄弟。 And 山舅肆考，角集, 4. 7b: 兩姨之子爲外兄弟，姑舅之子爲內兄弟。一說，⊙子稱姑子爲外兄弟，姑子稱舅子爲內兄弟。 The use of *nei* and *wai* is so confusing that even these encyclopaedists do not know which usage is correct. [The missing character is No. 16 on page 149.]

[24] During the sixth century the subject of *piao* relationships became so popular that even genealogies were compiled for them, e. g., *Wei shu* 高諒傳, 57. 5a: 諒造親表譜錄四十許卷，自五世以下，內外曲盡，覽者服其博記。

[25] *Li Chi* 大傳, 34. 7b: 四世而緦，服之窮也。

here we can only touch upon those fundamental aspects that are prerequisite to an elucidation of its influence upon the kinship system. *Chan ts'ui* (three years), *tzŭ ts'ui* (one year), *ta kung* (nine months), *hsiao kung* (five months), and *ssŭ ma* (three months) are commonly known as the *wu fu*, "five grades of mourning." Actually, the number is greater than five. The specifications of these grades have fluctuated much from period to period; certain grades have been dropped or added in conformity with the excentricities of particular periods. Although the specifications may thus have changed, the fundamental principles which underlie these specifications have remained constant.

All the paraphernalia expressed by the above terms [26] are mere accessories, the fundamental units of mourning being the "mourning periods." The basic unit is the *year*. All other degrees are either *chia lung* [increased mourning], or *chiang shai* [decreased mourning], relative to the basic unit. These principles are best expounded in the *San nien wên* of the *Li Chi*,[27] which says: "Why is it that the mourning period for the *nearest kin* is one year? Because the interaction of heaven and earth has run its round; and the four seasons have gone through their changes. All things between heaven and earth begin their processes anew. The rules of mourning are intended to resemble them." "Why should there be three years mourning [for parents]? The reason is to make it more impressive, *chia lung*, by doubling the period, so that it embraces two round years." [28] "Then why have the mourning of nine months? The reason is to prevent excessive grief." Therefore three years [actually twenty-five months counted as three years] is the highest expression, *lung*, of mourning. Three months and five months [29] are the lowest, *shai*. One year and nine months

[26] The terms *chan ts'ui, tzŭ ts'ui, ta kung, hsiao kung,* and *ssŭ ma* specify the kind of apparel to be worn at the mourning for a particular relative.

[27] 三年問, 58. 3a-4b. For translations in European languages, cf. J. LEGGE, *Lî Kî* Sacred Books of the East 28. 393-4; and S. COUVREUR, *Li Ki* [1913], 580-586.

[28] Twenty-five months are counted as three years, hence the "three years" mourning is only two years and one month.

[29] "Five months" are counted as two seasons, which should be six months. The substitution of five for six reflects an ancient Chinese aversion for even numbers. Thus, the basic periods are: three months (one season), five months (two season), nine months (three seasons), and one year (four seasons).

are the norms. Heaven above gives an example; earth below, a law; and man between, a pattern. The harmony and unity that should characterize men living in their kinships are hereby completely shown."

Mourning starts from the nearest kin with the basic unit of ch'i, one year. The nearest kin have three. According to the *Sang fu chüan*,[30] " the relation between father and son is one; between husband and wife is another; and between brothers is a third." With the three nearest kin, with the basic unit of ch'i, and with the principles of *chia lung* and *chiang shai*, the whole system is correlated with the kinship system as in Diagram IV (see p. 182).

The process is as follows: The mourning period for father is ch'i, one year; for grandfather, *ta kung*, nine months; for great grandfather, *hsiao kung*, five months; and for great great grandfather, *ssŭ*, three months. This is called *shang shai*, " ascending decrease." The mourning period for son is ch'i, one year; for grandson, *ta kung*, nine months; for great grandson, *hsiao kung*, five months; and for great great grandson, *ssŭ*, three months. This is called *hsia shai*, " descending decrease." The mourning period for brother is ch'i, one year; for father's brother's son, *ta kung*, nine months; for father's father's brother's son's son, *hsiao kung*, five month; and for father's father's father's brother's son's son's son, *ssŭ*, three months. This is called *p'ang shai*, " horizontal decrease."

The *chan ts'ui*, three years, mourning for father is *chia lung*, increased mourning; basically it is only one year. The one year, ch'i, mourning for father's father and father's brothers, is likewise *chia lung*, since basically it is the *ta kung* grade, nine months.

All non-sib relatives, whether consanguineal or affinal, are given the last grade of mourning, *ssŭ ma*, three months, no matter how closely related they may be.[31] They are subject also to the principle of *chia lung*; e. g., in the ancient mourning specifications, the mourning grade for mother's sister is *hsiao kung*, five months, but for the mother's brother it is only *ssŭ ma*, three months;[32]

---

[30] *I Li* 30. 8b-9a.

[31] *I Li* 喪服, 33. 2a: 外親之服皆緦也. Cf. *Jih chih lu* 5. 35-7.

[32] In modern mourning specifications mother's brother is increased to five months, *hsiao kung*.

the former is *chia lung*, and the latter is not. Basically they are all *ssŭ ma*.[33]

Mourning grades of a simpler kind must have existed long before the Chou period, but their elaboration began only when they fell into the hands of the Confucianists.[34] Using the family and sib as the bases for their ideological structure, these literati elaborated the mourning system with a view to the maintenance of sib solidarity. In the course of this elaboration of the mourning system they also standardized its basis, the kinship system, for a carefully graded system of mourning rites requires a highly differential kinship nomenclature, lest an awkward incommensurability ensue. This is especially apparent in the comparison of the *Êrh Ya* and the *I Li* systems. The *Êrh Ya* system, when compared with the system recorded together with the mourning rites [*Sang fu chuan*] in the *I Li*, is inconsistent and less differential in many respects. Certain classical scholars naively tried to amend the *Êrh Ya* with the *I Li* system, since they considered the *Êrh Ya* system below the standard of Confucian ideals of kinship.[35] They failed to see that the *Êrh Ya* represents an early state of the system, and the *I Li* a later but rationalized system worked over to conform with the mourning system.

There is no doubt that the *Êrh Ya* system was already to some extent rationalized through Confucian influences, but it is much less so than that in the *I Li*. With the Confucian ideals firmly implanted in the Chinese social structure from the second century B.C. on, the mourning rites were increasingly elaborated and popularized,[36] and concomitantly the kinship system, until both reached their apogée during the T'ang period.

The elaborate mourning rites are a distinctive feature of Chinese

[33] For the actual specifications one must consult the ritual works of each period. The above are merely general statements of principle.

[34] Certain scholars believe that the three-year mourning for father was a Shang custom, and that the Ju 儒, who practiced it during the Chou period and later evolved into Confucianists, were descended from the Shang dynasty people. Cf. Hu Shih: 說儒, 胡適論學近著, 第一集, 19-23, 90-94. For an opposite view cf. Fêng Yu-lan, The Origin of Ju and Mo, *CHHP* 10.279-310.

[35] Cf. 補正爾雅釋親宗族, by 鄭珍: *Ch'ao ch'ing ch'ao wên chi* 1.1a-4b.

[36] Cf. 三年喪服的逐漸的推行, by Hu Shih, op. cit., 95-102.

DIAGRAM IV[1]

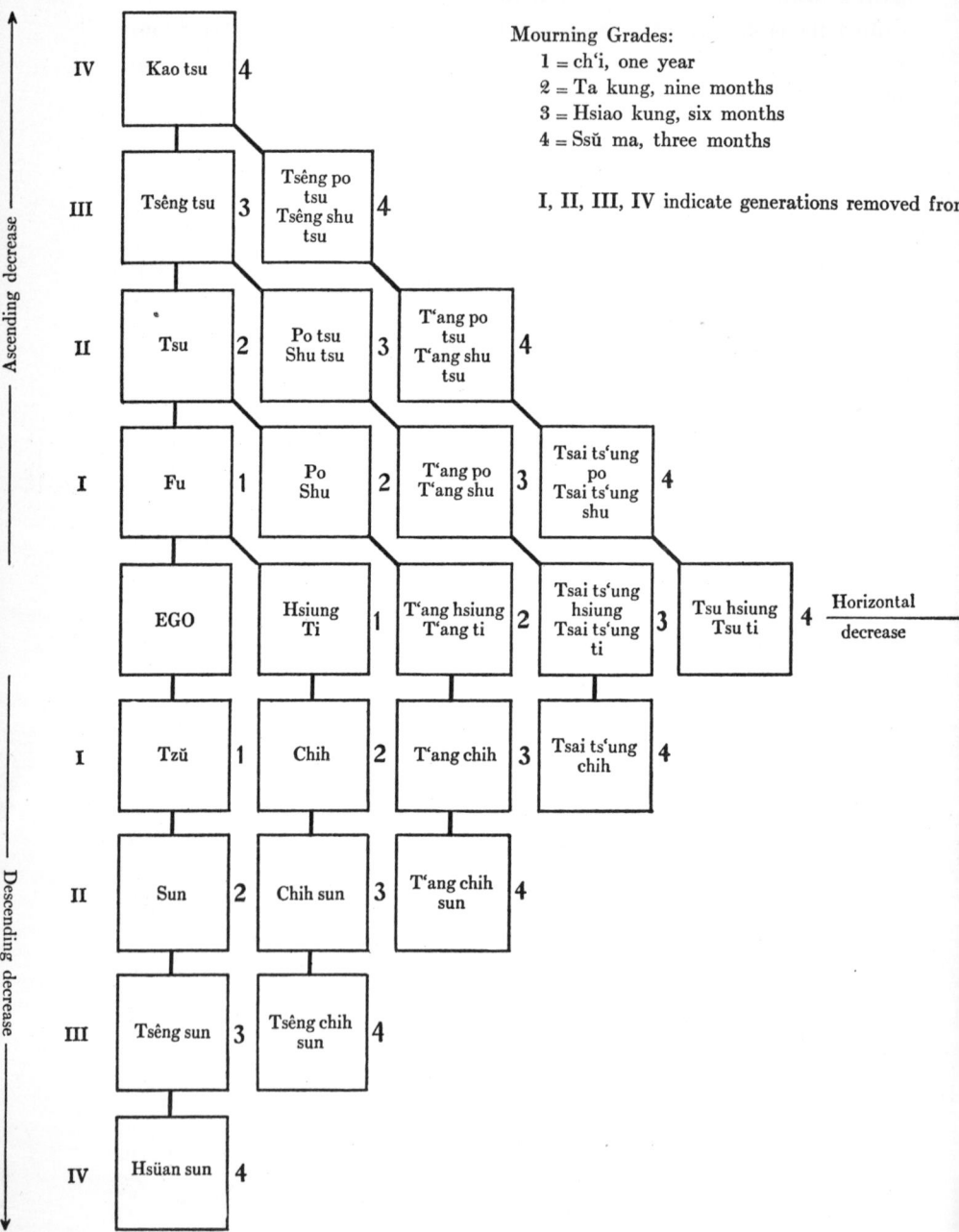

[1] Since the author is merely outlining the basic mourning system, only the male relatives are given. A complete specification would require eight to twelve diagrams.

ceremonial and social life. Under their influence the Chinese kinship system, through the increasing emphasis laid upon collateral differentiation and generation stratification, was transformed from a classificatory system based upon an exogamous sib organization into one of the descriptive type.[37]

Cross-cousin Marriages

Cross-cousin marriage is permitted, but not encouraged, in modern China. Generally, it is discountenanced not on the ground that the blood relationship is too close but on the ground that older relatives might be estranged as a result of difficulties which might arise between the young married couple, or vice versa. On the other hand, however, it is desirable, because it increases the number of relationships and knits the bond more closely.[38] Theoretically and ritually, it has been disapproved since the beginning of the first century A. D.[39] Legal prohibition, however, came rather late, the first definite clause being found in the Ming Code.[40] Since the enforcement of this law proved rather difficult,

---

[37] Kingsley DAVIS and W. Lloyd WARNER have made some very pertinent remarks concerning the use of "classificatory" and "descriptive" in connection with kinship analysis (Structural Analysis of Kinship, *American Anthropologist*, 39: 2 [1937], 291-315). They have also formulated a new set of categories for the structural analysis of kinship, with which, I think, few students will agree. The present writer disagrees with them in many points on their interpretation of the Chinese system. Since, however, this MS is going to press as their article appears, it is not possible to elaborate this remark.

[38] As the popular saying goes, 親上加親.

[39] *Pai hu t'ung*, 10. 16a: 外屬小功以上，亦不得娶也。是春秋傳曰，譏娶母黨也。袁準, of the Chin dynasty, says, [*T'ung Tien*, 60. 16b-17a, 內表不可爲婚議] 曰：今之人內外相婚，禮歟？曰：中外之親，近於同姓，同姓且猶不可，而況中外之親乎！古人以爲無疑，故不制也。今以古之不言，因謂之可婚，此不知禮者也. These statements probably read too much into the old ritual works.

[40] *Ming lü chi chieh*, 6. 17a: 若娶已之姑舅兩姨姊妹者，杖八十⊙並離異. The clause in the T'ang Code [*T'ang lü shu* 1. 14. 2b], 其父母之姑舅兩姨姊妹 • • • 並不得爲婚 • • • is sometimes expanded to include prohibition against cross-cousin marriage. Cf. *Jung chai sui pi* (*hsü pi*), 8. 12. The clause seems to indicate only parents' cross-cousins, not one's own cross-cousins; if so, the interdiction is against inter-generation marriage rather than cross-cousin marriage. But the *T'ung tien* (95. 11a) seems to show that during the T'ang period marriage with cross-cousins and mother's sister's daughter was actually prohibited.

in the Ch'ing Code this interdiction was invalidated by another clause, immediately following it, which allowed such marriages.[41] It must be noted that in modern China the kinship system is not the primary regulator of marriage; the important factor is sib exogamy supplemented by the generation principle. Thus, not only marriage with cross-cousin, but also with parallel cousin by mother's sister is allowed.[42] No statistical data for cross-cousin marriage are available at present, but my general impression is that the percentage is very small. In any event, cross-cousin marriage is in no way reflected in the modern kinship system.[43]

The ancient system as recorded in the *Êrh Ya* and the *I Li*

[41] G. JAMIESON: Translations from the General Code of laws of the Chinese Empire, Chapter 18: "A man cannot marry the children of his aunt on the father's side, or of his uncle or aunt on the mother's side, because though of the same generation they are within the fifth degree of mourning." But a little later in the *Li*, it reads: " . . . In the interest of the people it is permitted to marry with the children of a paternal aunt or of a maternal uncle or aunt." *China Review* 10 (1881-82), 83. Cf. also Sir G. T. STAUNTON, *Ta Tsing Leu Lee* (1810), 115.

[42] The practice of marriage with the mother's sister's daughter began at least as early as the third and fourth centuries A. D. E. g., *T'ung Tien* 95. 9a cites the discussion of 徐衆 of the Chin dynasty concerning the mourning obligations of dual relationship for mother's sister's daughter who married one's own older brother. A great many useless discussions have been lavished on this subject.

[43] T. S. CHEN and J. K. SHRYOCK in their "Chinese Relationship Terms," *American Anthropologist* 34: 4, 623-669, interpret in terms of cross-cousin marriage the fact that the father's sister's children and the mother's brother's children are designated by the same terms (see Chen-Shryock Table I, terms 85-92, and Table IV, terms 17-24, and note 33). But I do not see where the marriage element enters. The terms merely indicate cross-cousinship and nothing more. In order for these terms to be interpretable in terms of cross-cousin marriage, either the mother's brother or father's sister's husband must be addressed by the same term as that used for wife's father, or sister's husband or wife's brother addressed in cross-cousin terminology—in fact, any usage that will bring in the marriage element. Unfortunately, no terminology of this sort exists in the modern system. Hence, the authors' interpretations involving cross-cousin marriage in notes 33, 34, 39, 42, 61, 64, 65 and 67, are untenable. Furthermore, these interpretations are based on incomplete and faulty data. E. g., the important modifier *piao* is omitted from the terms of mother's sister's children, thus making mother's sister's daughters merge with wife's sisters. Mother's sister's children are *piao*, just as mother's brother's children and father's sister's children are *piao*. Not only cross-cousins are designated by *piao*, but also parallel cousins through mother's sister. This consideration completely invalidates the cross-cousin interpretation. Actually, since, as the authors have ably shown, the abandonment of the cross-cousin marriage custom was responsible for the development of the modern system, how can the modern system still be interpreted as indicative of that usage?

FACTORS AFFECTING THE SYSTEM

reflects a preferential type of cross-cousin marriage in certain kinship equations.[44] The terms concerned are the following: [45] Chiu 舅: a. mother's brother, b. husband's father,[46] c. wife's father, as *wai chiu*.[47] Ku 姑: a. father's sister, b. husband's mother, c. wife's mother, as *wai ku*. Shêng 甥: a. father's sister's sons, b. mother's brother's sons, c. wife's brother,[48] d. sister's husband (man speaking).[49] These terms indubitably manifest cross-cousin marriage of the bilateral type, coupled with sister exchange. The latter practice is shown especially in the term *shêng*, which means wife's brother and sister's husband.

Indirect evidence can be obtained from the arrangement of the *Êrh Ya*. Here the terms on kinship are arranged into four groups: i. Tsung tsu 宗族, Relatives through father. ii. Mu tang

---

[44] The first to interpret the *Êrh Ya* system in terms of cross-cousin marriage was M. GRANET, *La civilization chinoise*, 187. The thesis was further developed by Chen and Shryock, *op. cit.* 629-630.

[45] In the following notes some of the old Chinese interpretations of the extensions of these terms are given. They are not necessarily correct, but they do serve to show the traditional Chinese conceptions.

[46] The old interpretation of the extension of *chiu* and *ku* to include husband's father and mother is as follows: The one who is as venerable as father, but who is not the father, is mother's brother, *chiu*. The one to whom one is as attached as much as to mother, but who is not the mother, is father's sister, *ku*. Husband's parents are of similar relationship, hence we call them *chiu* and *ku*. Cf. *Pai hu t'ung*, 8.20b: 稱夫之父母謂姑舅何？尊如父而非父者，舅也．親如母而非母者，姑也．故稱夫之父母爲舅姑也．

[47] Wife's parents are called *wai chiu* (outside *chiu*) and *wai ku* (outside *ku*), that is to say, the wife is an outsider who comes to one's own family and makes it her own family too. She calls the husband's parents *chiu* and *ku*. The husband, in reciprocating, calls her parents *wai chiu* and *wai ku*, as a sign of equality for both parties. *Shih Ming*: 妻之父曰外舅，母曰外姑，言妻從外來，謂至己家爲歸，故反此義以稱之，夫婦匹敵之義也．

[48] Wife's brothers are called *wai shêng* (outside *shêng*) because their sister marries ego and becomes ego's wife, hence her male siblings are the *shêng* of an outside sib. *Shih Ming*: 妻之昆弟曰外甥，其姊妹女也，來歸己內爲妻，故其男爲外姓之甥．甥者，生也．他姓子本生於外，不得如其女來在己內也．

[49] Kuo P'o's commentary on the term *shêng*, in the *Êrh Ya*, says that these four individuals are of equal status, hence they reciprocally call one another *shêng*. 四人體敵，故更相爲甥．This conception of 敵體, equal status, between the relationships of *shêng*, has been the basis of most later interpretations; e. g., 姑之子爲甥，舅之子爲甥，妻之昆弟爲甥，姊妹之夫爲甥解，by 俞樾，詁經精舍自課文，春在堂全書本．

母黨, Relatives through mother. iii. Ch'i tang 妻黨, Relatives through wife. iv. Hun yin 婚姻, Relatives through husband. It is interesting to note that father's sister's sons, mother's brother's sons, sister's husband (M. S.), and sister's sons are all listed under Group iii, *ch'i tang*. The grouping of these relatives of quite distinct affiliations under *Relatives through wife* clearly demonstrates that the *Êrh Ya* system is built upon the practice of crosscousin marriage.

SORORATE

The sororate was operative during the feudal period, at least among the feudal lords.[50] The *Êrh Ya* gives the term for sister's husband [woman speaking] as *ssŭ*, literally "private." This is sometimes interpreted as evidence of the sororate, since a woman considers her sister's husband her "private."[51] The validity of this reasoning is rather dubious, without other terminological corroboration. *Ts'ung mu*, the term in the *Êrh Ya* and the *I Li* for mother's sister, has also been interpreted as a reflection of this usage. *Ts'ung mu* literally means "following mother."[52] But the term is best interpreted as a counterpart of *ts'ung fu*, a term for father's brother; hence *ts'ung* indicates the collateral line rather than potential motherhood.

Throughout the historical period, including modern China, the sororate has been practiced, but, since the possibilities are reduced by infant betrothal, its occurrence has been sporadic only. The

[50] Cf. M. GRANET, *La polygynie sororale et le sororat dans la Chine féodale*, 1920. The author overworks his material to arrive at forced conclusions, but most of the relevant data are collected in this little work. The thesis is also incorporated in his later work, *La civilization chinoise*, in which he has utilized the antiquated anthropological theory that the sororate and levirate represent survivals of an early fraternal group marriage.

[51] Cf. CHEN and SHRYOCK, *op. cit.*, 628. The *Shih Ming* interprets *ssŭ* in quite a different way. Female ego's sister's husband is called *ssŭ*, private, because this man has *private* relations with female ego's sister: 姉妹亙相謂夫曰私，言其夫兄弟之中，此人與己姉妹有恩私也. On the basis of this old interpretation, the *ssŭ* does not concern female ego at all, and so is scarcely evidence for the sororate.

[52] LIU Hsi (ca. 200 A. D.), in his *Shih Ming*, interprets *tsung mu* in the following manner: mother's sisters come to marry the father as *ti* 娣, hence they are of the status of *tsung mu*. Even if they do not marry the father, the term is still applied to them. This, I believe, is the earliest known sociological interpretation of kinship terminology. Whether or not it is correct is quite another matter.

single reflection in the modern system comes in the term *i*, which means mother's sister, father's concubine, wife's sister, and concubine. This identification seems irrefutable, yet another explanation is possible. A man calls his friends *hsiung*, older brother, and *ti*, younger brother, as a sign of courtesy and intimacy. A woman also calls her female friends *tzŭ*, older sister, and *mei*, younger sister, for the same reason. It is perfectly natural for the wife to call and consider her husband's concubines *mei*, and actually she does. The term *i* may thus be extended without recourse to the actual sororate at all. Similarly, *i* is usually used by children for the father's concubines,[53] and by servants for the master's concubines, in both instances as a complimentary term.

Where the sororate is practiced extensively, it may be accompanied by marriage with the wife's brother's daughter, because if the wife has no marriageable sister her brother's daughter is a good substitute. There are indications of such a practice in feudal China among the nobility.

When a feudal lord married, his bride was accompanied by eight bridesmaids called *yin*, who were his future concubines.[54] The *yin* were recruited in the following manner. The bride and the eight *yin* were divided into three groups, with three women in each group. The first group consisted of the bride, one of her younger sisters or younger half-sisters, *ti*,[55] and one of her older

[53] The *T'ung su p'ien* [18.17a-17b] states that the father's concubines are called *i*, because of the old *yin* marriage custom. *I* was originally a term for several sisters who married the same husband. In later times, the *yin* custom was discontinued but concubines are actually equivalent to the *yin*. Therefore, although father's concubines are not mother's sisters, *i* can still be applied to them. This sociological interpretation is rather erroneous. The *yin* marriage custom had nothing to do with the term *i*, and the *yin*'s were never called *i*, but always *chih* 姪 and *ti* 娣.

[54] *Kung-yang chuan* 莊公十九年, 8.1b-2a: 媵者何? 諸侯娶一國, 二國往 媵之, 以姪娣從. 姪者何? 兄之子也. 娣者何? 弟也.

[55] Whether *ti* 娣 meant the bride's actual younger sisters, or her younger half-sisters, i. e. her father's *yin*'s daughters, is a matter of speculation. Probably *ti* meant only her younger half-sisters, since there is abundant evidence to show that the daughters of the principal wife, *fu jên*, were always married out as *fu jên*, and *yin*'s daughters always married out as *yin*. In this way the noble-born and low-born were always kept constant 貴賤有常. This interpretation tallies with the uses of *i* and *ti* in the *Êrh Ya*. Cf. 毛際盛: *Shuo wên chieh tzŭ shu i* 說文解字述誼, (聚學 軒叢書本), 2.44a.

brother's daughters, *chih*. These three women constituted the principal group. Two other feudal states of the same sibname as the bride each supplied a principal *yin*, a *ti*, and a *chih*.[56] Thus there were three groups and nine women in all. The contribution to the *yin* by other states had to be entirely voluntary, and could not be solicited,[57] for it was not proper to ask children of others to become the dishonorable *yin*.[58]

This elaborate system for the selection of the *yin* served to insure a large number of descendants for succession in the feudal lord's office.[59] A niece, rather than a second younger sister was included in the *yin* in order to create a difference in the blood, so that if the two sisters failed to bear issue, a niece of different blood might bear a son. Similarly, the two other groups of *yin* were selected from two different states, in order that their blood would be still more dissimilar and the chances of having an heir would thus be tripled.[60] Sib relatives were selected for the *yin* with a view to preventing jealousy and intrigue within the harem.[61]

The *yin* custom was not strictly what is usually termed "secondary marriages." All the women were married at once, though if a *yin* were too young she could "wait her years in her parental state" until grown up, and was then sent to the bridegroom;[62] but this was rather unusual. In theory, a feudal lord

[56] *Tso Chuan* 成公十八年, 26.23a: 衞人來媵共姬，禮也。凡諸侯嫁女，同姓媵之，異姓否。 This may have been the general rule, but there were exceptions.

[57] *Kung-yang chuan* 莊公十九年, 8.2a: 何休注：言往媵之者，禮。君不求媵，二國自往媵夫人，所以一夫人之尊。

[58] *Pai hu t'ung*, 10.12a: 所以不聘妾者，何？人有子孫，欲尊之，義不可求人爲賤也 . . . 妾雖賢不得爲嫡。

[59] *Ibid.*, 10.11a: 天子諸侯一娶九女者何？重國廣繼嗣也。 *Ibid.*, 13b, 大夫成功受封，得備八妾者，重國廣嗣也。

[60] *Pai hu t'ung*, 10.11b: 不娶兩娣何？博異氣也。娶三國女何？廣異類也。恐一國血脈相似，以無子也。

[61] *Ibid.*, 備姪娣從者，爲其必不相嫉妬也。一人有子，三人共之，若己生之也。 *Kung-yang chuan*, 莊公十九年, 8.2a: 何休注：必以姪娣從之者，欲使一人有子，二人喜也。所以防嫉妬，令繼重嗣也。因以備尊尊親親也。

[62] *Kung-yang chuan* 隱公七年, 3.8a: 叔姬歸於紀。注：叔姬者，伯姬之媵也。至是乃歸者，待年父母之國也。

married only once in his life;⁶³ if the principal wife, *fu jên*, died a *yin* might act for the *fu jên* in her ceremonial and social capacities but could not assume the title of *fu jên*.⁶⁴ Actually, the *yin* had very little legal status, and were only " legalized mistresses " of the feudal lord.

The ministers, *ch'ing ta fu*, of the feudal lords could have one wife and two concubines, but could not take the wife's sisters or nieces as *yin*.⁶⁵ There are discrepancies in the interpretation of this rule in the classical works, and in a few instances the ministers followed the feudal lords' example and took the wife's younger sister and niece as concubines.⁶⁶ The scholar class, *shih*, i. e., the lower ruling class, were allowed one wife and one concubine.⁶⁷ Opinions differ as to whether or not this one concubine could be the wife's younger sister or niece. According to Ku Yen-wu (1613-1682), a scholar could not take his wife's younger sister or niece as concubine.⁶⁸ All commoners were allowed only one woman, at least in theory.⁶⁹

To judge from the evidence, the *yin* custom may have been only a kind of " legalized incest," whereby the emperor and feudal lords might assure themselves of an heir. Some of the lower nobility, however, might have followed suit later. It is not difficult to see why such a highly arbitrary custom could not have become very prevalent even among the nobility; not only was the supply of women limited, but the practice actually ran counter to the generation-principle ideology of this period. For example,

⁶³ *Ibid.,* 莊公十九年, 8.2a: 諸侯一聘九女, 諸侯不再娶.
⁶⁴ *Tso Chuan* 隱公元年, 2.2b-3a: 孟子卒, 繼室以聲子. 杜注: 諸侯始娶, 則同姓之國以姪娣媵, 元妃死則次妃攝治內事, 猶不得稱夫人, 謂之繼室. This rule was not absolute, cf. *Pai hu t'ung*, 10.18-19.
⁶⁵ *Pai hu t'ung*, 10. 17b: 卿大夫一妻二妾何? 尊賢重繼嗣也. 不備姪娣何? 北面之臣賤, 勢不足盡人骨肉之親也.
⁶⁶ E. g., *Tso Chuan*, 35.18a: 初臧宣叔娶於鑄, 生賈及爲而死, 繼室以其姪.
⁶⁷ *Pai hu t'ung*, 10.18a: 士一妻一妾何? 下卿大夫禮也. 喪服小記曰: 士妾有子, 則爲之緦.
⁶⁸ *Jih chih lu*, 5. 34b: 貴臣貴妾條.
⁶⁹ This is what was called 匹夫匹婦. In fact, under the feudal system, the title to all land was held by the feudal lord, and the common people worked under a " serf " system; no one could afford two women unless he belonged to the ruling class.

a feudal lord was not allowed to marry the noble women of his own estate, because, theoretically, everyone within his feudal state was his subject, and if the lord were married to any woman in his own state her parents would automatically be a generation higher than he and thus could no longer be his subjects. To avoid this contradiction, a feudal lord was required to marry outside his own state.[70] *Yin* marriage was swept away with the feudal system during the third century B. C. Since the beginning of the Western Han period [B. C. 206-A. D. 8], the practice has never again been recorded, either among the royalty or the nobility.[71]

When we turn to the ancient kinship system, we find there a peculiarity which seems to reflect the practice of marriage with the wife's brother's daughter. In the *Êrh Ya* sister's sons are called *chu* (M. S.). In a later passage, the same relative is called *shêng*. It has been remarked above, in connection with cross-cousin marriage, that in the *Êrh Ya*, *shêng* is principally used for father's sister's sons, mother's brother's sons, wife's brothers, and sister's husband (M. S.). This use of *shêng* to mean sister's sons does not comply very well with the generation principle stressed in the *Êrh Ya*.[72]

There is also a peculiar usage of *shêng* in the works of Mencius [B. C. 373-289]. Mencius used *shêng* to mean daughter's husband.[73] It seems that the overriding of the generation principle in the use of *shêng*, was a phenomenon that appeared rather late in the feudal period. *Shêng* was applied, during the feudal period, to 1. father's sister's sons; 2. mother's brother's sons; 3. wife's brothers; 4. sister's husband (M. S.); 5. Sister's son (M. S.); 6. daughter's husband.

The first four connotations can be interpreted in terms of cross-cousin marriage of the bilateral type, together with sister ex-

---

[70] *Pai hu t'ung*, 10.15a: 諸侯所以不得自娶國中何？諸侯不得專封，義不臣其父母．春秋傳曰：宋三世無大夫，惡其內娶也．

[71] Some students have even suspected that the *yin* marriage custom was a mere invention of the Han scholars.

[72] The only other term is the *Êrh Ya* which overrides generations, is *shu* 叔, for father's younger brother and husband's younger brother.

[73] *Mêng tzŭ*, 10A.10b: 舜尚見帝，帝館甥于貳室．．．．

change. The last two meanings seem to demand a cross-cousin marriage of the above type, together with a marriage with the wife's brother's daughter. In a case of this sort, both sister's husband and sister's son can marry ego's daughter, and ego's daughter's husband will be identified with both sister's husband and sister's son. However, in view of the fact that marriage with the wife's brother's daughter was only a " legalized incest " among the nobility and never a prevalent practice, teknonymy is a more plausible, and a simpler, explanation. Both sister's son and daughter's husband will be *shêng* to ego's own son, if cross-cousin marriage is assumed; ego simply adopts the son's term in addressing them.

On the whole, the influence of the sororate, both on the ancient and modern kinship systems, has been rather negligible. Insofar as the evidence goes, the sororate, both in ancient and modern China, is only a permissive type of marriage, that is to say, ego's marriage with one woman does not affect the status of marriage of her sisters, nor does it affect ego's own marriage status.

Levirate [74]

The junior levirate certainly exists in a few parts of modern China, at least among the poorer classes,[75] but, even in the few places where it is practiced, it is not considered respectable. A man adopts this only as a last resort in getting a wife. If necessary, he can sell his brother's widow and use the " bride-price " to

---

[74] Sir James Frazer has insisted upon the intimate co-existence of the sororate and the levirate (*Totemism and Exogamy*, 1910, 4. 139-150). R. H. Lowie also says: " The connection would undoubtedly appear to be even closer were not much of our information on marriage rules of primitive tribes of rather haphazard character. That is, it may safely be assumed that in not a few instances it is sheer negligence or defective observation that has made writers report one of the two customs without the other." (*Primitive Society*, 1920, p. 36.) If this correlation is valid, we should find the levirate in China as a correlative institution.

[75] Cf. *China Review*, 10 [1881-2], 71, The levirate in China. Also, Huang Hua-chieh 黃華節, Shu chieh sao 叔接嫂, *Eastern Miscellany*, 31: 7 [1934], 婦 20-21. P. G. von Möllendorff once remarked, " I have not been able to find the slightest trace of it (levirate), and it can never be of the same importance with the Chinese as with other people (e. g. to keep the family property), as posthumous adoption, the Chinese substitute for it, fully meets the object. *The Family Law of the Chinese* [1896], 17.

marry another woman. Legally, marriage with the older brother's or younger brother's widow is stringently prohibited;[76] the punishment is strangulation for both parties. G. Jamieson has doubted its existence in China at all under such heavy penalties.[77]

Whether or not the junior levirate existed in ancient China is quite problematical. Granet cites two cases from the *Tso Chuan*, but these can hardly be interpreted as evidence for the levirate.[78] Chên and Shryock say that "the relationship terms indicates only the junior levirate, in which an older brother marries his deceased younger brother's wife. A wife calls her husband

---

[76] This law was first explicitly stated in the *Ming lü chi chieh* 6. 20, promulgated during the period Hung-wu, 1368-1398 A. D. (latest revision, 1610 A. D.). In all earlier codes the levirate was prohibited under a more general clause, e. g., in the *T'ang lü shu i*, 14. 3a: 諸嘗爲祖免親之妻而嫁娶者，各杖一百．緦麻及舅甥妻、徒一年．小功以上以姦論．妾各減二等，並離之．Under this clause, the levirate is out of the question.

On the other hand, the explicit clause in the Ming Code against the levirate may be a reaction to its introduction into China through the Mongols of the Yüan dynasty. Cf. 李魯人：元代蒙古收繼婚俗傳入內地之影響．大公報，史地周刊, No. 8, April 10, 1936, (Sheet 11), p. 3.

[77] *China Review* 10. 83 says: "In view of the severe penalty for it, it is scarcely possible that the levirate can be practiced in any part of China."

[78] *La civilisation chinoise*, 424-5. The two cases cited are: Pi Wu-ts'un [LEGGE, *Chinese Classics*, V: ii, 773]; Tzŭ Yüan and Hsi Kuei [*Ibid.*, V: i, 115]. In the first case, Pi Wu-ts'un, who was going to war and intended to marry a woman of better status, refused his father's proposal on the pretext that his father would be able to marry his younger brother to the woman in question. The woman proposed by his father not only cannot be regarded as his wife, but not even as his fiancée. In the second case, Tzŭ Yüan already had the full authority of the state of Ch'u, and did not need to marry his older brother's widow in order to acquire his brother's authority, as Granet's theory demands. On the other hand, Hsi Kuei was a noted beauty and Tzŭ Yüan's attempted seduction was motivated by lust. Unfortunately for Granet's thesis, Tzŭ Yüan did not succeed in seducing her, and was soon killed.

According to the ancient mourning specifications, sister-in-law and brother-in-law are not subject to mourning obligations, hence Granet considers his hypothesis confirmed inasmuch as relatives without mourning obligations may marry. But mere mourning obligations do not prevent marriage, e. g., cross-cousins have mourning obligations to each other but, according to Granet's theory, they are prescribed to marry!

What we need are actual instances of the levirate—not this ambiguous and anomalous kind of material which may be interpreted to support any kind of hypothesis. Granet is laboring to use the sororate and levirate as proof of an earlier fraternal group-marriage which is in itself a hopeless hypothesis.

and her husband's older brother (possible husbands) by the same term, *po*, but uses a different term for his younger brother." [79] The authors are somewhat confused in this. Where only the older brother can marry the younger brother's widow, the practice is termed the "senior" levirate, *not* the "junior" levirate. The "senior" levirate alone is not found in Asia. Either both forms of the levirate are practiced by the same people, or the junior levirate alone is practiced, as in India, southeastern Asia, and northeastern Asia. There is also an anachronism in the connotations of *po* cited by the authors. In a few places in the "Book of Odes," *po* is interpreted as meaning husband,[80] but this usage is not found in literature after 500 B.C. On the other hand, the use of *po* to mean husband's older brother did not begin until the tenth century A.D.[81] Thus, *po* meaning husband and *po* meaning husband's older brother not only are not contemporaneous, but are separated by a hiatus of fifteen centuries! Historically minded though the Chinese may be, I do not see how one can interpret this terminology in terms of the levirate.

Chattopadhyay has interpreted the differentiation of older and younger brothers in India in terms of the junior levirate.[82] Such an interpretation is extremely weak, unless supported by other terminological corroboration. If the junior levirate explains the differentiation of older and younger brothers, it certainly does not explain the differentiation of older and younger sisters, which is

---

[79] CHÊN and SHRYOCK, *op. cit.*, 628-29.

[80] *Shih Ching*, 3C. 7a-8b: 伯兮朅兮，邦之桀兮；伯也執殳，爲王前驅．自伯之東，首如飛蓬，豈無膏沐，誰適爲容 . . . . The *po* used here is sometimes interpreted as meaning husband, but it is uncertain whether *po* is a relationship term for husband, or a reference to the official title the husband holds, or simply a word meaning "the brave and handsome one." To judge from the context, the last is the preferable interpretation.

[81] T'AO YO 陶岳, *Wu tai shih pu* 五代史補 (豫章叢書本), 5.8a: 【李】濤爲人不拘禮法，與弟瀚雖甚雍睦，然聚話之際，不典之言，往往間作．瀚娶禮部尚書竇寧固之女，年甲稍高，成婚之名，竇氏出參濤，輒望塵下拜．瀚驚曰：大哥風狂耶？新婦參阿伯，豈有答禮儀？濤應曰：我不風，只將是親家母．

[82] CHATTOPADHYAY, Levirate and Kinship in India, *Man*, 22 (1922), 25. W. Lloyd WARNER, Kinship Morphology of Forty-one North Australian Tribes, *American Anthropologist* 35.66 makes a similar interpretation.

also characteristic of most Indian systems. Whether or not the *tsung fa* adequately explains the expression of the category of age in generation in the Chinese system, as advocated by the old Chinese authors, we do not know; certainly this expression cannot be explained by the junior levirate, which is of so sporadic occurrence in China.

Teknonymy

We have already discussed several types of marriages that are relevant to the determination of minor kinship peculiarities. With the exception of cross-cousin marriage, the influence of the others, both on the ancient and modern systems, has been rather negligible. These problems will be further discussed here in connection with teknonymy and other peculiarities in the system, in order to ascertain the actual determining factor or factors.

As has already been shown, generation is an important structural principle in the Chinese system. It also regulates marriage among relatives, and plays an important rôle in the functioning of Chinese social and ceremonial life as a whole, since the dealings between relatives are in many respects based upon generation differences, so also in the assignment of mourning grades, etc. Since generation is such an important factor in the system, we should expect it to be consistently expressed in terminology. Yet there are some notable exceptions. Mother's brother and wife's brother are designated by the same term, *chiu*; mother's sister and wife's sister by the same term, *i*; father's older brother and husband's older brother by the same term, *po*; father's younger brother and husband's younger brother by the same term, *shu*; father's sister and husband's sister by the same term, *ku*; etc. These peculiarities are of significance, because originally the generations of these relatives were clearly differentiated by distinct terms, and only in the course of time were they gradually merged into each other.

First, let us take the connotations of the term *chiu*, and the terms for the wife's brother, during the various periods, and arrange them in a single table, as follows:

Period	Connotations of *chiu*	Terms for wife's brother
I 1st Millennium B.C.	mother's brother husband's father wife's father	*shêng*
II 1st Millennium A.D.	mother's brother	*fu hsiung ti*
III 2nd Millennium A.D.	mother's brother wife's brother	*chiu*

The various connotations of the term *chiu* in Period I are perfectly intelligible from the point of view of cross-cousin marriage, as discussed above. In such a marriage, the mother's brother and husband's father is the same person, so also the mother's brother and wife's father. In Period II the cross-cousin marriage was dropped, and consequently the meaning of *chiu* became confined to mother's brother.

The terms for the wife's brother are different for each of the three periods. In Period I wife's brother was called *shêng* 甥. *Shêng* also meant, in this period, father's sister's son, mother's brother's son and sister's husband (man speaking).[83] This is also explicable in terms of cross-cousin marriage of the bilateral type, coupled with sister exchange. In Period II, because of the disappearance of this type of marriage, *shêng* was no longer applicable to any of these relatives and new terms were introduced to take its places. *Fu hsiung ti* is the term used for wife's brother.[84]

In Period III the term *chiu* (mother's brother) was extended to include wife's brother. The first use of *chiu* in this new meaning is to be found in the *Hsin T'ang Shu*. In the biography of Chu Yen-shou, we read: " Yang Hsing-mi's wife is the older sister of Chu Yen-shou. . . . Hsing-mi [luring Chu Yen-shou into a

---

[83] Cf. *Êrh Ya*.
[84] The term is purely descriptive. *Fu* 婦 means wife, *hsiung ti* means brother (older and younger). *Pei Ch'i Shu* 崔昂傳, 30. 9b-10a: 崔昂直臣、魏收才士、婦兄⊙夫, 俱省罪過. *Ibid.*, 鄭元禮傳, 29. 6b: 但知⊙夫, 疏於婦弟. *Ch'i hsiung ti* 妻兄弟 and *nei hsiung ti* 內兄弟 were also permissible at this time. Cf. Table III. [From this point the editors have been forced to substitute the symbol ⊙ for some frequently recurring characters. In this instance the missing characters are No. 11 on p. 149.]

trap] says, 'I have lost my eyesight and my sons are too young. Having *chiu* [meaning Chu Yen-shou] take my place, I shall have no worry.' "[85] This is certainly a curious extension of the use of *chiu*, for, through all the previous vicissitudes of the term, the generation element had always been preserved. This overriding of the generation principle certainly warrants an explanation.

A strictly sociological interpretation would point to a marriage with the wife's brother's daughter. In Period I *chiu* also meant father-in-law; since, in this interpretation, the wife's brother is a potential father-in-law, the extension of the term *chiu* to include him would be perfectly logical. However, there are several difficulties in such an interpretation. In the first place, historical evidence does not seem to support this hypothesis. Wife's brother's daughter marriage in connection with the *yin* custom was never a preferred form, nor, as stated above, was it common even among the feudal nobility. Moreover, it disappeared together with the feudal system during the third century B. C., and has never been practiced since. Secondly, *chiu* had ceased to mean wife's father at least a thousand years before it was extended to mean wife's brother. These two temporal considerations, involving a hiatus of more than a millennium, are irreconcilable with such an interpretation. Thirdly, such a marriage contradicts the generation principle; wife's brother's daughter is one generation lower than ego; and thus, in the Chinese system, is within the incest group. Legally, inter-generation marriage between all relatives became definitely prohibited at least half a millennium before *chiu* was extended to mean wife's brother.[86] In the face of these objections, the above interpretation is untenable.

It is significant that Chinese scholars had been employing teknonymy to explain this terminological anomaly long before the introduction of the term into anthropological discussion by

[85] *Hsin T'ang Shu* 朱延壽傳, 189. 10a: 田頵之附全忠，延壽陰約曰：公有所爲，我願執鞭。頵喜。二人謀絶行密。行密憂甚，紿病目，行觸柱、僵。妻，延壽姊也，掖之. 行密泣曰：吾喪明，諸子幼，得⊙代，我無憂矣。[The missing character is No. 16 on p. 149.]

[86] The T'ang Code, compiled and promulgated during the period A. D. 627-683, stringently prohibits inter-generation marriage: *T'ang lü shu i* 13. 2.

E. B. Tylor.[87] Ch'ien Ta-hsin [1727-1804], one of the most penetrating classical scholars of his time, attributed this extension of the meaning of *chiu* to the gradual, imperceptible effect of the practice of teknonymy.[88] Wife's brothers are *chiu* to one's own children. The father, adopting the language of his children, also calls his wife's brothers *chiu*. This process can clearly be seen in the above-mentioned instance of Chu Yen-shou. Yang Hsing-mi called Chu Yen-shou *chiu*, at the same time mentioning his own sons. One can infer that, after long tcknonymous usage, the term *chiu* established itself and finally displaced the older term.

Whether or not this hypothesis can be sustained depends upon the additional evidence we can adduce for its support, or, in other words, upon whether or not it can explain all the peculiarities of the same nature in the system. Let us now turn to the examination of those terms by which the wife addresses her husband's brothers: *po* for the husband's older brother, and *shu* for the husband's younger brother. But *po* was originally a term for father's older brother, and *shu* for father's younger brother. This overriding of generations is quite aberrant, from any point of view. Insofar as I am aware, there is no social or marital usage in China, nor is there any comparable usage that ethnographic data suggest, which could give rise to such a terminology.

From the historical point of view, the terms for these relatives were different at different periods. In the *Êrh Ya* the father's older brother is called *shih fu*. From the second century B. C. down to the present *po fu* has been the standard term, but from the fourth century A. D. on, *po* alone also has been in use.[89]

In the *Êrh Ya* husband's older brother is called *hsiung kung*.[90] During the succeeding centuries *hsiung chang* was commonly em-

---

[87] On a Method of Investigating the Development of Institutions . . . , *Journal, Anthropological Institute*, 18 (1889), 245-69.

[88] *Hêng yen lu*, 3.13b: 予按... 後世妻之兄弟獨得舅名，蓋從其子女之稱，遂相沿不覺耳．

[89] *Li Chi* 曾子曰, 18.10a: 已祭而見伯父叔父. *Yen shih chia hsün* 風操篇 2.6b: 古人皆呼伯父叔父，而今世多單呼伯叔. Cf. *Hêng yen lu*, 3.6-7.

[90] 夫之兄爲兄公．

ployed.⁹¹ Ca. the tenth century A. D. *po* was extended to include husband's older brother.⁹²

In the *Êrh Ya* the father's younger brother is called *shu fu*. This term has continued in use without any radical change down to the present; as in the case of *po*, above, from the fourth century A. D. on *shu* alone has also been in use. *Shu* is also used in the *Êrh Ya* for husband's younger brother. This usage is rather unusual, inasmuch as it overrides generations and thus contradicts its own statement of principle, that " husband's siblings are affinal siblings." ⁹³

As has been stated above, no possible explanation for this blending of generations can be found in marriage forms; the only possible alternative is teknonymy. Husband's brother's are *po* and *shu* to female ego's own children. The mother, adopting the terminology of her children, also calls them *po* and *shu*. This case tremendously strengthens our hypothesis, since no other known social factor or form of marital relationship can adequately explain these usages.

A similar situation exists in the terminology for father's sister and husband's sister, both called *ku*, and mother's sister and wife's sister, called *i*.

As has already been pointed out, *ku* is used in the *Êrh Ya* for father's sister, husband's mother, and wife's mother [e. g., *wai ku*], as a result of cross-cousin marriage. When cross-cousin marriage declined, *ku* was usually employed for father's sister alone. In the *Êrh Ya*, husband's older sister is called *nü kung*, and younger sister *nü mei*.⁹⁴ Somewhat later *shu mei* was used for the husband's younger sister.⁹⁵ In the fourth century A. D. the term *ku* began to be extended to include husband's sisters.⁹⁶ The factors

[91] *Shih Ming*: 夫之兄 ... 俗間曰兄章. Cf. Table IV, term 5.
[92] See p. 193, note 81.
[93] *Êrh Ya*: 婦之黨爲婚兄弟, ⊙之黨爲婣兄弟. [The missing character is No. 18 on p. 150.]
[94] 夫之姊爲女公, 夫之女弟爲女⊙. [No. 11 on p. 149.]
[95] *Hou Han Shu* 曹世叔妻【班昭】傳, 114. 8b: 婦人之得意於夫主, 由⊙姑之愛己也; ⊙姑之愛己, 由叔⊙之譽己也. [First and second are No. 16; last, No. 11 on p. 149.]
[96] The earliest occurrence of the term *hsiao ku* for husband's sister is in the famous

behind this extension cannot be exactly ascertained, although the marriage rules and social customs of the period concerned are fairly well known. The extension could not have been due to marriage with the wife's brother's daughter, in which case the husband's sister would be elevated to the position of the husband's father's sister; the above-cited objections to a similar interpretation of *chiu* also apply here. Furthermore, other features do not follow either terminologically [97] or conceptually.[98] Teknonymy remains the best explanation since husband's sisters are *ku* to female ego's own children.

Originally *i* was used, as in the *Êrh Ya*, for wife's sisters. In the *Êrh Ya* mother's sisters are called *ts'ung mu*. The earliest use of *i* to mean mother's sister is found in the *Tso Chuan*. In the twenty-third year [B. C. 550] of Duke Hsiang, a passage reads, "*I*'s daughter of Mu Chiang." [99] By checking the relatives connected with Mu Chiang, one finds that the term, *i*, here does not mean wife's sister [or married sister, woman speaking] as it should, but mother's sister. As a matter of fact, the passage should read, "*ts'ung mu*'s daughter of Mu Chiang," not, "*i*'s daughter."

Theoretically, the sororate, together with a marriage with the father's widows, would adequately explain the usage. In this combined type of marriage, the father marries mother's sisters and

poem 古詩爲焦仲卿妻作 (*Yü t'ai hsin yung chi*, 1. 17b): 却與小姑別，淚落連珠子。新婦初來時，小姑始扶牀，今日被驅遣，小姑如我長。 The literature on the dating of this poem has already become enormous. Hu Shih tends to date it earlier than most others, about the middle of the third century A. D., cf. 現代評論, 6: 149. 9-14: 孔雀東南飛的年代. Others tend to date it much later, about the fourth and fifth centuries A. D.

[97] E. g., among the Miwok, where marriage with the wife's brother's daughter is reflected in twelve terms [E. W. GIFFORD, *Miwok Moieties,* University of California Publications in American Archaeology and Ethnology, 1916, p. 186], but these are all lacking in the Chinese system.

[98] Among the Omaha, marriage with the wife's brother's daughter is reflected in the conceptual identification of the father's sister, the female ego, and the brother's daughter [A. LESSER, Kinship Origins in the Light of Some Distributions, *American Anthropologist* 31 (1929), 711-12], but it is not indicated in the terminology. In the Chinese system the generations of father's sister, husband's father's sister, and the husband's sister are clearly distinguished conceptually, although the terminology fails to differentiate them.

[99] *Tso chuan* 襄公二十三年, 35. 18a.

ego marries wife's sisters. Ego again marries father's widows after his decease. Then mother's sisters become equated with wife's sisters. This explanation seems fantastic but has some support, since a man's secondary wives (concubines) may also be called *i*, i. e., mother's sisters, wife's sisters, and secondary wives are all grouped in one class. It is well known that the sororate was practiced among the feudal nobility, but, as regards the inheritance of father's widows, there is no authenticated evidence.[100] Indeed, such a marriage would have been abhorrent to the ancient Chinese. We learn that the old writers detested the Hsiung-nu, pastoral nomads of the northern steppes, who married their fathers' widows, and never failed to mention this as an excuse for derision.[101]

K'ung Ying-ta [A. D. 574-648] explained the extension of *i* to include mother's sister (ts'ung mu) as due to the psychological similarity between these relatives.[102] Mother's sister's are *i* to one's father, just as wife's sisters are *i* to oneself. The son, imitating the language of his father, also applies *i* to his father's *i*. In short, this case seems to demand a psychological explanation, together with reverse teknonymy.

The connotations of *shên* are likewise of significance. Father's

[100] M. Granet cites the case of Duke Hsüan [718-700 B. C.] of Wei who married his father's concubine I Chiang (*La civilisation chinoise*, p. 401). Apparently, Granet is not aware of the fact that Ku Tung-kao 顧棟高 [1679-1757] has convincingly shown that I Chiang had not previously been Duke Hsüan's father's concubine (*Ch'un ch'iu ta shih piao* 春秋大事表, 清經解 ed., 50. 3a-4b: 衞夷姜晉齊姜辨). Even if it be admitted that this is an authentic instance of step-mother and step-son marriage, nothing is proved thereby, since the instance is quite anomalous. Not only are such anomalies recorded in quite a few instances from the Ch'un Ch'iu period, but also examples of incest, involving actual blood relationship, like grandmother and grandson, brother and sister, cf. 王士廉：左淫類記. But Granet has omitted these. Indeed, such anomalies are always cropping up in Chinese history, even in quite recent times, e. g., the T'ang Emperor Kao-tsung [650-684] married his father's concubine Wu Chao 武曌 later known as the notorious Empress Wu of the T'ang dynasty, and the Emperor Hsüan-tsung [712-756] married his son's concubine Yang Yü-huan, well-known to Europeans as the foremost beauty of China. One wonders how Granet would interpret these instances.

[101] *Shih Chi* 匈奴列傳, 110. 2a: 父死妻其後母，兄弟死皆取其妻妻之. The Hsiung-Nu customs of marrying father's widows other than one's own mother and the levirate were so well known to the ancient Chinese that they frequently mentioned them as a sign of the moral inferiority of the Hsiung-nu.

[102] *Tso Chuan* 襄公二十三年, 35. 18a.

younger brother's wife and husband's younger brother's wife are both called *shên* in the vocative. In the *Êrh Ya* father's younger brother's wife is called *shu mu*, which is the standard term today. *Shên* first came into use during the Sung period; it is usually regarded as a contracted pronunciation of *shih mu*.[103] Its extension to include husband's younger brother's wife was effected about the same period.[104] No possible marital relationships could give rise to such an equation of relatives, nor could any other sociological factor. Teknonymy offers the simplest solution. Husband's younger brother's wife is the *shên* of female ego's children.

The origin of the terms *kung*, for husband's father, and *p'o*, for husband's mother, has never been investigated. The old term for husband's father is *chiu*, and for husband's mother, *ku*, both of which reflect cross-cousin marriage. During the first millennium A. D. a large number of terms were introduced for the designation of these two relatives, since *chiu* and *ku* were no longer applicable after the discontinuance of that particular type of marriage, but *kung* and *p'o* finally gained prevalence.[105]

On the other hand, *kung* and *p'o* are prevalent grandparent terms.[106] Why the wife should apply grandparent terms to the husband's parents is rather perplexing. This terminology is most susceptible to marital irregularities, but we cannot see what marital form, no matter how startling, could be involved here. But if we assume teknonymy, the situation immediately explains itself.

The foregoing cases comprise the most significant terminological anomalies, and constitute about all the instances in the Chinese system, both ancient and modern, where the generation principle is openly violated. In every case we have tried to explain these exceptions by facts and hypotheses which have proved illuminat-

[103] *Ming tao tsa chih*, 13b: 王聖美嘗言，經傳無嬸字 ... 考其說，嬸字乃世母二字合呼也. *Shih mu*, pronounced as one word, became *shim*, or *shên*.
[104] *Tzŭ wei tsa chi* 紫薇雜記, of Lü Tsu-ch'ien 呂祖謙, 1137-1181 A.D. [*Shuo fu* 說郛, 19] 2a: 呂氏舊俗，母母受嬸房婢拜，以受其主母拜也. 嬸見母母房婢妮，即答拜，是亦毋尊尊之義也 ... 母母于嬸處自稱名，或去名不稱新婦，嬸于母處則稱之. *Mu mu* is used in the sense of husband's older brother's wife, and *shên* in the sense of husband's younger brother's wife.
[105] See Table IV, terms 1 and 2.
[106] See Table I, terms 13 and 14.

ing in the discussion of analogous phenomena elsewhere. But we have found none of them applicable to the Chinese situation; rather, we have found teknonymy the only satisfactory explanation.

There can be no doubt that teknonymy is the determining factor in all these cases, but one may ask whether teknonymy is universal in China and of sufficient antiquity to have been involved in producing such effects in kinship terminology. The universality of this practice in China is unquestionable; the frequency of its use, however, might have varied in time and place. At times the practice was so accentuated that the ordinary forms of address became hardly intelligible.[107] In many regions, e. g., Wusih, Kiangsu, the bride ordinarily addresses her husband's relatives as if she were one generation lower. The teknonymy practiced is usually of the type that omits the child's name, just as in English a man may call his wife simply "mother." This type is especially efficacious in producing the irregularities just discussed.

As regards the antiquity of teknonymy, we must depend upon historical evidence. The earliest instance that can be interpreted as teknonymy is recorded in Kung-yang's commentary on the *Spring and Autumn Annals* [Ch'un Ch'iu]. In the sixth year of Duke Ai [B. C. 489] is recorded an instance concerning Ch'ên Ch'i. He, in referring to his wife, says, "The mother of Ch'ang...."[108] Ch'ang is known to have been Ch'ên Ch'i's son. The teknonymous usage here is indubitably clear. This instance, in the fifth century B. C., is more than a millennium earlier than most of the cases we have discussed above, except those involving *i* and *shêng*, which

---

[107] E. g., the extreme instance of the practice of teknonymy in South China, as recorded in the *Ch'ing hsiang tsa chi* 青箱雜記, by Wu Ch'u-hou 吳處厚 ca. 1080 A. D. [涵芬樓 ed.] 3. 2b-3a, of the Sung period, which reads: 嶺南風俗相呼不以行第, 唯以各人所生男女小名呼其父母. 元豐中 [1078-1085], 余任大理丞, 斷賓州 [modern 賓陽縣 in Kwangsi] 奏案, 有民韋超, 男名首, 卽呼韋超作父首. 韋遜男名滿, 卽呼韋遜作父滿. 韋全【男】女名插娘, 卽呼韋全為父插. 韋庶女名睡娘, 卽呼庶作父睡, 妻作嬸睡.

[108] *Kung-yang chuan* 哀公六年, 27. 12a: 諸大夫皆在朝, 陳乞曰: 常之母, 有魚菽之祭, 願諸大夫之化我也.

are about contemporaneous. On the other hand, if we make allowance for the conservative spirit of the classical writers in recording colloquial language, it is reasonable to infer that teknonymy is much older than this documentary evidence would indicate.

The influence of teknonymy on kinship terminology is quite apparent. Gifford, in discussing similar usages in the English and Californian kinship terminologies, has cogently remarked: " There must be, in other kinship systems, many analogous cases [cases analogous to the English teknonymy of calling husband " daddy " and wife " mother "], some of them crystallized into invariable custom like the Luiseño case, cases which require no startling form of marriage for their explanation, but which could be readily understood as our own, if we were but familiar with the family of the group in question." [109]

In the very limited literature on teknonymy, various theories have been put forth to account for its origin, but no serious attempt has been made to use it in explanation of other social phenomena. Teknonymy as a usage is based on kinship and kinship nomenclature—a circumlocutory way of expressing embarrassing relationships. Through long and intensive use, why should it not have produced certain peculiarities in kinship terminologies, as other social usages are reputed to have done? The Chinese cases are especially illuminating. It would require a series of marital or other special practices to explain the peculiarities of *chiu, po, shu, ku, i, shên, kung, p'o* and *shêng*, whereas they can uniformly be explained by the single principle of teknonymy.

[109] *Californian Kinship Terminologies* 265. In the Chinese instances the situation is so apparent that even so amateur an observer as Hart has been led to remark: " The nomenclature employed in the designation of two brothers-in-law and two sisters-in-law, i. e., by a wife toward the brothers and sisters of her husband, and by a husband toward the brothers and sisters of his wife, seems to have its origin in the names applied to such people by the children (their class children, or nephews and nieces) born of the marriage. Thus an individual's wife's brother is the *kew* [= *chiu*] of that individual's children, and that individual in speaking of him as his brother-in-law, employs the same word, *kew*, to designate him as such, so with the other." [MORGAN, *Systems* . . . , p. 413.] Morgan, however, engrossed in his evolutionary " stage building," entirely overlooked this pertinent remark.

HISTORICAL REVIEW OF TERMS

The Chinese method of counting relationships starts with the three nearest kin, i. e., parent-child, husband-wife, and brother-sister, and extends out in all directions. Whenever one comes to the question of Chinese kinship extensions, one always stumbles upon the problem of *chiu tsu* 九族, "nine grades of kindred." This is a much discussed but vague term, which first occurs in the *Book of History*.[1] Its interpretation comprises two major theories, representing two different schools of classical commentators. The Modern Script School interprets the *chiu tsu* as follows: The four groups of relatives of the father; plus the three groups of relatives of the mother; plus the two groups of relatives of the wife.

The four groups of relatives of the father are: 1. With ego in the center, counting four generations above, four generations below, and the four collateral lines each counting four generations from the lineal line from males through males. 2. Father's sisters, when married, and their descendants. 3. Ego's sisters, when married, and their descendants. 4. Ego's daughters, when married, and their descendants.

The three groups of relatives of the mother are: 5. Mother's father and mother. 6. Mother's brothers. 7. Mother's sisters.

The two groups of relatives of the wife are: 8. Wife's father. 9. Wife's mother.

This interpretation is not followed by the Ancient Script School of classical commentators, who believe the *chiu tsu* includes only the sib relatives but not the non-sib relatives. Therefore, according to their interpretation, the *chiu tsu* takes into account only the first of the above nine groups of relatives. That is, the *chiu*

---

[1] *Shu Ching* 堯典, 2.7b: 以親九族. Whether this is the earliest use of the term or not is very questionable, since the antiquity and authenticity of the 堯典 is much questioned. However this is the focal point of later controversies. 顧頡剛 has a very penetrating discussion of the *Problem of Chiu tsu* 九族問題, in 清華週刊 37: 9-10, 105-111.

tsu means simply nine " generations," viz., the four ascending and the four descending generations, with *ego* in the middle. Naturally, because of the collective responsibility of the individual's social actions, many students tend to narrow down the interpretation in order to lessen the social and legal complications. The *chiu tsu* problem, however, is purely an academic and historical matter.

In the present work the classification of the *Êrh Ya* is generally followed. The actual extent of the terminology listed, however, is entirely dictated by the needs of modern research and by the material available, although all those relatives within the Chinese mourning grades are included. The sib relatives are emphasized, but such emphasis is unavoidable in a system based strictly upon a patrilineal social grouping, where many of the terms for non-sib relatives are merely extended combinations from those for sib relatives.

The relatives are divided into two main groups and subdivided into four tables. The two main divisions are Consanguineal Relatives and Affinal Relatives. Under Consanguineal, there is a subdivision into Relatives through Father and Relatives through Mother; and under Affinal, into Relatives through Wife and Relatives through Husband. Under each group are also listed persons connected through marriage, that is the " in-law's "; this is a conventional practice.

In the tables the modern standard terminology is given first under each entry; these terms represent the system as it now stands. The slight variant combinations in some of the compounded terms have been carefully collated against one another from contemporary sources. In collating, two criteria were adopted: the statistical and inferential; i.e., if two or more forms are equally common, that form inferentially most in keeping with the working principles of the system is given as the standard form, and the others are given as alternatives. These variations are rather insignificant, and, in view of the number of people using the system and the geographical extent of the system, quite inevitable.

Under each standard term are given the historical terms in their chronological order. Their exact nature, whether alternative, literary, or dialectical² is indicated, together with their modern status.³ Following them come the referential and vocative terminologies. If no terms are given, it is understood that they can be formed from previously stated formulae. No stereotyped order is followed, but generally the treatment varies according to the nature of the material and in keeping with special circumstances.

Citations illustrating the use of terms are given in the notes. It is possible only to give citations for the earliest occurrence of a new term, or for an old term used in a new meaning. In some cases, the most typical instances are cited. These citations are of importance, since only through them can the exact nature and chronology of a term be determined.

In the tables I have attempted to record as fully as possible the whole range of terms.⁴ Thus, under the father's father no less than twenty terms are given, under various usages and periods, and in some instances the number is still greater. Of course, not all terms can be so treated, especially terms for distant relatives, which are compounded from the basic terminologies, but the slight variations in any possible combinations are given. A full recording of the whole nomenclature and the determination of the exact nature of each term are indispensable conditions for the proper understanding and interpretation of the system, since most of the early misunderstandings are the result of partial and mixed renderings of the system comprising forms from different strata of the terminology.

---

² Dialectical differences in Chinese kinship terminology have been somewhat exaggerated. Many of them are mere local variations in pronunciation which do not affect the morphology of the system.

³ I. e., the exact connotation and nature of the term in modern usage, if it is still used.

⁴ Terms that are idiosyncracies and have no general currency are excluded. E. g., the Emperor Hsüan of the Northern Chou dynasty did not like others to use the term *kao*, so he changed the term *kao tsu* to *chang tsu*, and *tsêng tsu* to *tz'ŭ chang tsu*: *Pei shih* 周宣帝紀, 10. 32a: 又不喜聽人有高者, 大者, ... 改 ... 九族稱高祖者為長祖, 曾祖為次長祖. Terms of such nature will not be considered

Consanguineal Relatives—Table I

Relatives Through Father

I. Generation of the father's father's father's father

1. Kao tsu fu 高祖父 ffff

In the Classics *kao tsu* was sometimes used to mean any ancestor ascending from grand-father.[1] In the 17th year of Duke Chao [525 B. C.] in the *Tso Chuan*, the first ancestor was called *kao tsu*.[2] In another place the ninth ancestor was referred to as *kao tsu*.[3] King K'ang [1078-1053 B. C.] called King Wên and King Wu *kao tsu*, but actually they were his great-grand- and grand-fathers.[4] Apparently, during the Chou period, if the actual father's father's father's father is meant, *wang fu* must be added, like the *kao tsu wang fu* used in the *Êrh Ya*. The term *kao tsu* does not occur in the mourning relations of the *I Li*[5] and it is surmised that any lineal relative ascending from *tsêng tsu* may be called *tsêng tsu*.[6]

During the T'ang period *kao mên*[7] was used, but infrequently; it was most likely a posthumous term. The posthumous and

---

[1] *Jih chih lu*, 24. 1a: 漢儒以曾祖之父爲高祖, 考之於傳, 高祖者, 遠祖之名爾.

[2] *Tso chuan* 昭公十七年, 48. 5a: 郯子曰 . . . 我高祖少皞摯之立也 . . .

[3] *Ibid.*, 昭公十五年, 47. 11b: 王曰 . . . 且昔而高祖孫伯黶司晉之典籍, 以爲大政, 故曰籍氏. The term 高祖 is meant for the ninth ancestor of 籍談 It is also used in the same way in the *Shu Ching*, e. g., 盤庚 9. 17a: 肆上帝將復我高祖之德. The term *kao tsu* refers to Ch'êng T'ang (1765-1760 B. C.?).

[4] *Shu Ching*, 康王之誥, 19. 3a: 無壞我高祖寡命.

[5] In the 喪服傳 of the *I Li*, since there are no mourning specification for ffff, the term for him does not occur. In the ritual works, the first use of *kao tsu* for ffff is in the 喪服小記 of the *Li Chi*, 32. 7b: 有五世而遷之宗, 其繼高祖者也.

[6] *Mêng ch'i pi t'an*, 3. 3a: 喪服但有曾祖曾孫, 而無高祖玄孫. 曾, 重也. 自祖而上. 皆曾祖也; 自孫而下, 皆曾孫也; 雖百世可也. Very probably the use of *kao tsu* for ffff, and *tsêng tsu* for fff is due to the development of the sib organization of the Chou period but originally both of them meant simply "distant ancestors." Cf. 丁山: 宗法原考, *CYYY*, 4: 4 (1934), 399-415, in which he considers that during the Shang and early Chou periods, exact relationships are only counted to two generations both above and below.

[7] *Chin shih ts'ui pien* 段行琛碑, 101. 11b: . . . 高門平原忠武王孝先, *Ch'êng wei lu*, 1. 4a, 按高門, 高祖也.

temple term used in the *Li Chi* is *hsien kao*.⁸ The term is no longer used in this sense. Since the Yüan dynasty (1280-1367) *hsien kao* had been used as an epitaphic term for father.

2. Kao tsu mu 高祖母 f f f m

Kao tsu wang mu 高祖王母 is the term used in the *Êrh Ya*.

3. Kao tsu ku mu 高祖姑母 f f f f si

Kao tsu wang ku 高祖王姑 in the *Êrh Ya*.

4. Kao tsu ku fu 高祖姑父 f f f f si h

No term is given in the *Êrh Ya*. In tracing relationship through women of the father's sib married out, the terms for these women are usually employed; the terms for their husbands, only infrequently.

II. Generation of the father's father's father

5. Tsêng tsu fu 曾祖父 f f f

As a form *tsêng tsu* may be used alone. *Tsêng tsu wang fu* is the term used in the *Êrh Ya*. *Tsêng ta fu*,⁹ *ta wang fu* ¹⁰ and *wang ta fu* ¹¹ have been common alternative terms since the sixth century A.D. *Tsêng mên* ¹² was commonly used during the T'ang

---

⁸ *Li Chi* 祭法, 46.8a-9: 顯考廟. 疏: 曰顯考廟者, 高祖也. *Ibid.*, 檀弓, 9.12a-13: 殷主綴重焉. 鄭注: 綴, 猶聯也. 殷人作主而聯其重, 縣諸廟也; 去顯考乃埋之. 孔疏: 顯考, 謂高祖也.

⁹ *Shih chi* 夏本紀, 2.1b: 禹之父鯀, 鯀之父帝顓頊, 顓頊之父曰昌意 ... 禹之曾大父昌意及⊙鯀, 皆不得在帝位. *Ch'ang-li chi* 崔評事墓銘, 24.1b: 曾大父知道.... [Here and in two following notes supply No. 4, on p. 149.]

¹⁰ *Chü-chiang wên chi* 裴光庭碑, 19.3b: 大王⊙定....

¹¹ *Chin shih yao li* 書祖⊙例, 7b: 庚承宣為田布碑, 稱曾祖為王大父.

¹² *Hsin T'ang shu* 孝友程袁師傳, 195.6b: ... 改葬曾門以來, 閱十二年乃畢. *Chin shih ts'ui pien* 比邱尼惠源誌銘, 82.13a-19b: 曾門梁孝明皇帝 ... Chien Ta-hsin [*Chien yen t'ang chin shih wên po wei*, 6.13] says: 稱曾祖為曾門, 未詳其義. From what can be deduced from the evidence, *mên* 門 was a very common posthumous term in referring to lineal relatives from the second ascending generation and upward during the fourth to the eighth centuries A.D. Father's father was called 大門中, father's father's father's father was called 高門, so father's father's father was called 曾門. Its origin may be similar to the term 從兄弟門中 as explained by Yen Chih-t'ui. See p. 222, note 132.

period. All these terms may be used posthumously. The ancient posthumous term is *huang kao*,[13] as used in the *Li Chi*. *Huang kao* was later used as a posthumous term for father, but has been prohibited since the Yüan dynasty, since *huang* implies "imperial."

The vocative is rather variable. *T'ai wêng*[14] and *tsêng wêng*[15] were common from the fourth to the ninth century A.D. *Wêng* means "venerable old man." *T'ai kung* and *t'ai yeh yeh*[16] are common modern vocatives.

6. Tsêng tsu mu 曾祖母 f f m

In the *Êrh Ya*, *tsêng tsu wang mu*. The most common modern vocative is *t'ai p'o*, or *t'ai p'o p'o*.[17]

7. Tsêng po tsu fu 曾伯祖父 f f f o b

Tsu tsêng wang fu is used in the *Êrh Ya*, and *tsu tsêng tsu fu* in the *I Li*.[18] Both these terms also apply to father's father's father's younger brothers.

8. Tsêng po tsu mu 曾伯祖母 f f f o b w

In the *Êrh Ya*, *tsu tsêng wang mu*, and correspondingly *tsu tsêng tsu mu* in the *I Li*. Both these terms also apply to father's father's father's younger brother's wife.

9. Tsêng shu tsu fu 曾叔祖父 f f f y b

The vocatives of 7 and 9 are similar to 5, but differentiated by prefixing their numerical order or titles.

---

[13] *Li Chi* 祭法, 46.8a-9: 曰皇考廟. 孔疏. 曰皇考廟者, 曾祖也.

[14] *Nan Shih* 齊廢帝鬱林皇紀, 5.1a: 太翁.

[15] 曾翁. Since *wêng* was commonly used as vocative for grandfather, *tsêng wêng* and *t'ai wêng* were used for great grandfather. *Wêng* may also be used for any venerable old man.

[16] 太公 and 太爺爺. *T'ai* means "great." *Kung* and *yeh yeh* are vocatives for grandfather; *t'ai kung* and *t'ai yeh yeh*, for great grandfather.

[17] 太婆 or 太婆婆. *P'o* or *p'o p'o* are vocatives for grandmother; *t'ai p'o*, for great grandmother. K'UNG P'ing-chung 孔平仲, ca. 1080 A.D., 朝散集, 豫章叢書 ed., 2.19a: 代小子廣孫寄翁翁. 太婆八十五, 寢膳近何似?

[18] *I Li* 喪服, 33.6a: 族曾祖⊙母. 鄭注: 族曾祖父母者, 曾祖昆弟之親也.

10. Tsêng shu tsu mu 曾叔祖母 f f f y b w

The vocatives of 8 and 10 are similar to 6, but differentiated by prefixing their sibnames or their husband's numerical order.

11. Tsêng tsu ku mu 曾祖姑母 f f f si

Tsêng tsu wang ku is the term used in the *Êrh Ya*. Modern vocative, *ku t'ai p'o*.

12. Tsêng tsu ku fu 曾祖姑父 f f f si h

Modern vocative, *ku t'ai kung* 姑太公 or *ku t'ai yeh* 姑太爺.

III. Generation of the father's father

13. Tsu fu 祖父 f f

Tsu may be used alone to mean father's father, but it may mean any ancestor.[19] In the *Êrh Ya*, *tsu* was used synonymously with *wang fu*,[20] but *wang fu* is now more often used in the posthumous sense. Since the Han period *ta fu*[21] has been frequently used. Other early alternative terms, like *tsu chün*,[22] *tsu wang fu*[23] and *tsu wêng*,[24] are commonly met in literature. Another common early term is *kung*,[25] which in many localities is still used as a vocative.[26] Since *kung* is a common complimentary term for any older man, its connotation as a relationship term is indefinite. It is used to mean father, husband's father, etc. *T'ai kung*[27] is used in the *Hou Han Shu* to mean father's father, but is now used as a vocative for father's father's father.

[19] *Jih chih lu*, 24.1a: 自父而上，皆曰祖. 書微子之命曰, 乃祖成湯是也.
[20] *Êrh Ya*: 祖, 王⊙也.
[21] *Shih Chi* 留侯世家, 55.1a: 留侯張良者, 其先韓人也. 大父開地 . . . . Ibid. 鄭當時傳, 120.6b: 然其知交皆其大⊙行.
[22] *K'ung ts'ung tzŭ* 居衞篇, 2.45b: 子思旣免, 曰 . . . 祖君屈於陳蔡作春秋.
[23] *Chin shih ts'ui pien* 王文幹墓誌, 113.62a: 奉天定難南朝元從功臣諱英進, 公之祖王父也.
[24] 樂清縣白鶴寺鐘款識有祖翁祖婆之稱. Cf. *Ch'êng wei lu*, 1.7a.
[25] *Lü shih ch'un ch'iu*, 10.10a: 孔子之弟子從遠方來者, 孔子荷杖而問之曰: 子之公不有恙乎?
[26] Cf. *Ch'êng wei Lu*, 1.8a.
[27] *Hou Han Shu* 李固傳, 93.14b: 姊文姬【固女】 . . . 見二兄歸 . . . 曰:

The most common modern vocatives are *yeh yeh* 爺爺, *kung kung* 公公, *a wêng* 阿翁, *wêng wêng* 翁翁.[28] Their usage depends upon local custom.

The depreciatory term is *chia tsu* or, uncommonly, *chia kung*. The prefixing of *chia* to *tsu* to refer to one's own father's father dates from the Han period. It is sometimes condemned as incorrect and vulgar,[29] but is nevertheless in universal usage today.

The complimentary term is *tsun tsu fu*.[30] *Ta mên chung*[31] was used as a complimentary term during the fifth or sixth century A. D. It was most probably a posthumous term, and is not used today.

The ancient posthumous terms were *wang kao*[32] and *huang tsu kao*.[33] The former was probably more often used in connection with ancestral temples, and the latter, with sacrifices. This minute distinction might be due to the important rôle of ancestral worship and sacrifices in the sib organization during the feudal period. During the fifth century A. D. *hsien wang chang jên*[34] was commonly used. None of these terms is used today. The modern posthumous terms are *hsien tsu* 先祖 or *wang tsu* 亡祖.

14. Tsu mu 祖母 f m

The term in the *Êrh Ya* is *wang mu* 王母, which corresponds to *wang fu*. Later terms, like *ta mu*[35] and *tsu p'o*,[36] more or less

李氏滅矣! 自太公以來，積德累仁，何以遇此? During the Han period, *kung* was sometimes used for father; *t'ai kung*, for father's father.

[28] *Shih shuo hsin yü*, 3B. 10a.
[29] Cf. *Yen shih chia hsün* 風操篇, 2. 4b-5b.
[30] *Ibid.*, 2. 5a-b: 凡與人言，稱彼祖⊙母，世⊙母，⊙母及長姑，皆加尊字. 自叔以下，則加賢字，尊卑之差也. [Supply No. 4, p. 149.]
[31] *Ibid.*, 2. 6a: 大門中.
[32] *Li Chi* 祭法, 46. 8a-9b: 曰王考廟. 孔疏: 曰王考廟者，祖廟也.
[33] *Ibid.* 曲禮, 3. 22a: 祭王⊙曰皇祖考，王母曰皇祖妣.
[34] *Yen shih chia hsün* 書證篇, 6. 15b: 今世俗呼其祖考爲先亡丈人，又疑丈當作大.
[35] *Hsin shu* 俗激篇, 3. 1b: 今其甚者，到大⊙矣，賊大母矣. *Han shu* 文三王傳, 47. 5b: 共王母曰李太后，李太后清平王之大祖也. 顏師古注: 大母，祖母也.
[36] 祖婆; see p. 210, note 24.

correspond to the terms for father's father. The depreciatory term is *chia tsu mu*, and the complimentary term, *tsun tsu mu*. The ancient posthumous term is *huang tsu pi*,[37] and the modern term, *hsien tsu mu*. *T'ai p'o* was once used as a vocative for father's mother but it is now used for father's father's mother. The most common modern vocatives are *p'o p'o* 婆婆 [38] and *nai nai* 嬭嬭.[39]

15. Po tsu fu 伯祖父 ffob

Both the *Êrh Ya* and *I Li* give the term *ts'ung tsu tsu fu*.[40] It applies to both older and younger brothers of father's father.

Po wêng[41] is a modern vocative. The vocatives of 13 may also be applied here by prefixing the numerical order or title.

16. Po tsu mu 伯祖母 ffobw

Ts'ung tsu tsu mu is the term both in the *Êrh Ya* and the *I Li*.[42] Since the *Êrh Ya* also gives the term *ts'ung tsu wang mu* 從祖王母, in can be inferred that during the Chou period father's father's brothers may also have been called *ts'ung tsu wang fu*. During the Han period it was abbreviated to *ts'ung tsu mu*.[43] *Po p'o*[44] is a more modern term, and may be used vocatively.

17. Shu tsu fu 叔祖父 ffyb

Compare 15. In the *Kuo Yü* the term *ts'ung tsu shu mu*[45] is used for father's father's younger brother's wife. It can be inferred that in ancient times *ts'ung tsu shu fu* may also have been

---

[37] *Li Chi* 曲禮, 3.22a: 王母曰皇⊙妣.

[38] K'UNG P'ing-chung 朝散集, *op. cit.*, 代小子廣森寄翁翁, 2.19a: 婆婆到輦下, 翁翁在省裏.

[39] *Ch'in shu chi* 1.6b: 嬭, 按今讀奴蟹切, 曰嬭嬭. 或以呼母, 或以呼⊙母, 或似呼伯叔母. 嬭 is also written 奶. It originally meant mother and was read *ni*, as in the *Kuang yün*, 嬭, 楚人呼母.

[40] *I Li* 喪服, 33.1a: 從⊙⊙⊙母.

[41] 伯翁, cf., 龔大雅, 羲井題記 in *Pa ch'iung shih chin shih pu chêng*, 117.12a-14b.

[42] Cf. note 40.

[43] *Li Chi* 檀弓, 9.25b: 敬姜曰: 婦人不飾. 鄭注: 敬姜者, 康子從⊙⊙.

[44] 伯婆.

[45] *Kuo yü* 魯語, 5.12a: 公⊙文伯之母, 季康子之從⊙叔母也.. [First missing character is No. 4, p. 149.]

used for father's father's younger brother, and *ts'ung tsu shih fu* for father's father's older brother, but this inference is by no means certain. Since the T'ang period *shu wêng*[46] has been a common alternative term, and may be used in the vocative. The vocatives of 13 may also be applied here, according to local usage, by prefixing the numerical order.

18. Shu tsu mu 叔祖母 f f y b w

Compare 16 and 17. In the Han dynasties *chi tsu mu*[47] seems to have been used. According to another interpretation, *chi tsu mu* means father's father's brother's secondary wives,[48] but there is no means of checking this. Since the T'ang period *shu p'o* seems to have been a common vocative. *P'o p'o* may be used in the vocative for 16 and 18 by prefixing the numerical order of their husbands, or their own sibnames.[49]

19. Ku tsu mu 姑祖母 f f si

Wang ku 王姑 is the term given in the *Êrh Ya*.

20. Ku tsu fu 姑祖父 f f si h

21. Chiu tsu fu 舅祖父 f m b

Chiu tsu[50] may be used alone. The inverted form *tsu chiu*[51] was used quite early; and *ta chiu*[52] was used during the Later Han period.

22. Chiu tsu mu ○○母 f m b w

---

[46] *Ch'ang-li chi*, 23.13a: 祭李氏二十九娘子文. Han Yü refers to himself as 十八叔翁 and to his wife as 十八叔婆. *Ibid.*, 23.12b: 祭潓文, where he refers to himself as 十八翁 and to his wife as 十八婆. They were offering sacrifice to his brother's grandchildren.

[47] *Chin shih ts'ui pien* 18.1b: 收養季○母.

[48] CH'IEN Ta-hsin says [*Ch'ien yen t'ang chin shih wên po wei*, 1.26b] that 其稱季○母, 猶言庶○母也. [Supply *tsu*, ancestor.]

[49] *Yen shih chia hsün* 風操篇, 2.7b: ○母之世叔母, 皆當加其姓以別之.

[50] *Lêng lu tsa shih* 冷廬雜識, by LU I-t'ien 陸以湉, ca. 1850 A.D. 筆記小說大觀 ed. 2.25b: 今之稱謂 ... 稱○之○爲○○. [Supply *fu* ... *chiu* ... *chiu-tsu*.]

[51] *Chin shu* 應詹傳, 70.1b: 鎮南大將軍劉弘, 詹之○○也.

[52] *Hou Han Shu* 張禹傳, 74.2a: ○○況, 族姊爲皇祖考夫人 ... 況 ... 見光武, 光武大喜曰: 今乃得我大○乎! [Supply *tsu-fu*.]

23. I tsu mu 姨祖母 f m si

24. I tsu fu ○○父 f m si h

The vocatives for the above can be constructed from the vocatives for grandparents, whatever forms are used, by prefixing *ku*, *chiu* and *i*.

25. T'ang po tsu fu 堂伯祖父 s of 7 or 9 > f f

26. T'ang po tsu mu ○○○母 w of 25

27. T'ang shu tsu fu 堂叔祖父 s of 7 or 9 > f f

28. T'ang shu tsu mu ○○○母 w of 27

No term is given for 25 and 27 in the *Êrh Ya*, but *tsu tsu wang mu* 族祖王母 is used for 26 and 28. It is inferred that *tsu tsu wang fu* may have been used for 25 and 27. In the *I Li*, *tsu tsu fu* is used for 25 and 27, and *tsu tsu mu* for 26 and 28,[53] whereas in the *Êrh Ya* these terms are used for the son and the son's wife of either 25 or 27. The *I Li* is simply using an abbreviated form.

Vocatives of 15-18 may be applied here, respectively.

29. T'ang ku tsu mu 堂姑祖母 d of 7 or 9

In the *Êrh Ya*, *tsu tsu ku*. This term is rather inconsistent with the whole *Êrh Ya* system, since logically it should be *tsu tsu wang ku*. Perhaps the *Êrh Ya* was already beginning to use abbreviated forms.

30. T'ang ku tsu fu 堂姑祖父 h of 29

Vocatives can be built up by prefixing grandparent vocatives with *ku*, and can further be differentiated by prefixing the numerical order of 29, or the sibname of 30.

31. Piao tsu fu 表祖父 f f f si s

32. Piao tsu mu ○○母 w of 31

The above two terms can be further differentiated by prefixing *ku*, *chiu* and *i*, e. g., *ku piao tsu fu* for f f f si s, *chiu piao tsu fu* for f f m b s, *i piao tsu fu* for f f m si s. Ordinarily, *piao tsu fu* is

---

[53] *I Li*, 33. 6a.

applied to them all. Usually these relationships are not continued socially after the death of the f f f si and f f m, unless it be that either of the parties strongly wishes to maintain them. Terms for their descendants will not be given in this table. If the relationships are maintained, terms could easily be constructed, e.g., the sons of 31 will be called *t'ang piao po fu* and *t'ang piao shu fu*, etc.

IV. Generation of the father

33. Fu 父 father

Fu is primarily a standard literary term throughout, and is seldom used alone as a vocative. *Wêng*[54] was an old vocative. A *kung*[55] and *tsun*[56] were prevalent from the third to the sixth centuries A. D. About the fifth century A. D. members of some of the royal families called father *hsiung hsiung*,[57] a term for older brother. During the T'ang dynasty the royal family called father *ko*,[58] nowadays a universal vocative for older brother. Before this, *ko* had never been used in either of these senses.[59] It might be that *ko* was an old dialectical term for father, and that during this period it became confused with *hsiung*, thereupon losing its original meaning of father and acquiring the connotation of " older brother," but the matter is most perplexing.

[54] *Shih chi* 項羽本紀, 7.26a: 漢王曰 . . . 吾翁即若翁.
[55] *Nan Shih* 顏延之傳, 34.4b: . . . 又非君家阿公. According to 王念孫 [*Kuang ya shu chêng*] 公 and 翁 are very similar in sound and may be dialectical renderings of a same term.
[56] *Sung shu* 謝靈運傳, 67.30a: 阿連才悟如此, 而尊作常兒遇之. *Shih shuo hsin yü* 品藻篇, 2B.30a: 劉尹至王長史許清言, 時荀子年十三, 倚牀邊聽. 既去, 問⊙曰, 劉尹語何如尊? *Ibid.* 9b: 謝太傅未冠, 始出西詣王長史清言, 良久, 去後荀子問曰: 向客何如尊? [Supply *fu*.]
[57] *Pei Ch'i shu* 南陽王綽傳, 12.6b: 兄兄.
[58] *Chiu T'ang shu* 王琚傳, 106.16b: 元宗泣曰: 四哥仁孝. The *ko* is meant for the Emperor 睿宗. *Ibid.* 棣王琰傳, 107.5a: 惟三哥辯其罪. The 三哥 is here used by 琰 in referring to his father, Emperor Hsüan-tsung. *Ko* was also used by the royal family of the T'ang dynasty to refer to oneself before the son. *Ch'êng hwei lu*, 1.15a: states: 淳化閣帖唐太宗與高宗書稱哥哥勅. ⊙ 對子自稱哥哥, 蓋唐代家法如是. [Supply *fu*.]
[59] 哥 is defined in the *Shuo wên* as " to sing," or " a song."

Yeh 耶 is a vocative used from the sixth century A. D. on;[60] it is also written 爺.[61] *Tieh* 爹,[62] which may be a later variant pronunciation of *t'o* 爹,[63] a dialectical form of western Hupeh of about the same period, is now a common vocative. *Pa pa* is almost as commonly used as *tieh*; it first occurred in the *Kuang Ya*, which reads, "*pa* ... is father."[64] The *Cheng tzŭ t'ung* considers *pa* a term of the southern aborigines,[65] and states that the aborigines call their elders *pa pa* 八八, or *pa pa* 巴巴, and that the Chinese lexicographers added the classifier 父 to form 爸. On the other hand, *pa* is also considered a later variant pronunciation of *fu* 父.[66]

The dialectical difference, insofar as the evidence goes, seems to indicate that *tieh* is predominantly a northern usage,[67] and *pa*, a southern;[68] but this explanation is by no means certain.

The *Kuang Yün* states that the people of Wu call father *chê*,[69] but according to the *T'ung Ya* father was called *lao hsiang* in Wu.[70] None of these terms seem to be in use today. The in-

[60] *Yen shih chia hsün* 文章篇, 4.10b.
[61] *Nan shih* 侯景傳, 80.22b: 王偉勸立七廟 ... 並請七世諱 ... 景曰：前世吾不復憶, 惟阿爺名摽. The original form is 耶, and 爺 is a later form with classifier No. 88 added. For discussion cf. *Kai yü ts'ung k'ao*, 37.15; *Hêng yen lu*, 3.2; and *Ch'êng wei lu*, 1.15-16.
[62] *Ch'ang-li chi* 祭女挐女文, 23.14a: 阿爹阿八, 使汝妳 ... 祭于第四小娘子之靈. Cf. *Shu p'o*, 1.2b-3a, 呼⊙爲爹.
[63] *Kuang ya*: 爹 ... ⊙也, pronounced *t'o*. *Nan shih* 始興忠武王憺傳, 52.15b: 詔徵以本號還朝, 人歌之曰: 始興王, 人之爹【徒我反】赴人急, 如水火, 何時復來哺乳我. 荊土方言謂⊙爲爹, 故云. For discussion cf. *Kai yü ts'ung k'ao*, 37.15.
[64] 爸 ... ⊙也.
[65] *Chêng tzŭ t'ung*: 爸. The Miao and Yao tribes of southwest China still call father *pa*, or its slight variants. Cf. *Miao fang pei lan* 苗防備覽 by Yen Ju-i 嚴如熤 [1843 紹義堂 ed.] 8.6a, 9.2b, and 9.10a; *Ling piao chi man* 嶺表紀蠻 by Liu Hsi-fan 劉錫藩 [1932, Shanghai, Commercial Press] 137.
[66] Chêng Chên (*Ch'in shu chi*, 1.1b) says that 古讀巴如迪, 卽⊙之重唇音, 逐作巴加⊙. 今俗呼⊙或爲巴巴, 或爲粑粑, 或爲八八, 並此字.
[67] *Kuang yün*: 爹, 北人呼⊙.
[68] *Chi Yün*: 爸, (部可切, 又必駕切) 吳人呼⊙. The *Ch'êng wei lu*, 1.27a: also states that 吳俗稱⊙爲阿伯. *Po* 伯 may be a different rendering of *pa* 爸.
[69] 奢 (正奢切), 吳人呼⊙. The modern pronunciation is the same of *yeh* 爺.
[70] *T'ung ya* 稱謂, 19.4b.

habitants of Fuchow call father *lang pa* 郎罷;⁷¹ this usage dates from the T'ang period. Before that, *lang* alone also had the meaning of father;⁷² hence *lang pa* may be combination variant of *lang* and *pa*. In modern usage in that place, however, *lang pa* is always used in the referential and never in the vocative.

Fu ch'in 父親 ⁷³ may be used as a literary vocative by the son in addressing his father, as in a letter. In this connection, *ta jên* 大人 ⁷⁴ and *ch'i hsia* 膝下 ⁷⁵ must be appended, making the term *fu ch'in ta jên ch'i hsia*, a stereotyped form of literary address. In addressing letters, *ch'i hsia* is used for either parent, whereas *ta jên* may be appended to any term for relatives of higher generations. *Ch'i hsia* is primarily a literary parent term; its literal meaning is "like a child at your knees."

The father, in referring to himself before his children, may use *nai kung* 乃公,⁷⁶ *nai wêng* 乃翁 ⁷⁷ and the more colloquial and modern terms *a tieh*, *a pa*, or *lao tzŭ* 老子. In certain localities *lao tzŭ* may also be used for father in general.⁷⁸

The depreciatory term is *chia fu*, or *chia yen*.⁷⁹ *Yen* literally means "the stern and respected one." *Chia chün* ⁸⁰ is also fairly common. *Chia kung* ⁸¹ is a rather uncommon old term.

⁷¹ *Hua yang chi*, 1.13a: 囝, 哀閩也. 自注. 囝, 音蹇, 閩俗呼子爲囝, 呼 ⊙爲郎罷. 郎罷別囝, 吾悔汝生. . . .

⁷² *Shu I*, 1.9b: 古人謂⊙爲阿郎. *Pei shih* 汲固傳, 85.4a: 【李】憲卽爲固長育, 至十餘歲. 恆呼固夫婦爲郎婆. According to 朱⊙ [cited by *Ch'êng wei lu*, 1.26a] 蓋北朝稱⊙⊙郎也.

⁷³ *Ch'in* 親 means "relative," "parent."

⁷⁴ 大人 literally means "big man," that is "senior." It is frequently used alone as a vocative, e. g., *Shih Chi* 越世家, 41.11b; *ibid.*, 高祖本紀 8.32a.

⁷⁵ *Hsiao Ching* 聖治章, 5.4b: 故親生之膝下以養⊙母 . . . 注: 膝下, 謂孩幼之時也.

⁷⁶ *Han Shu* 陳萬年傳, 66.17a: 萬年嘗病, 命咸教戒於牀下. 語至夜半, 咸睡, 頭觸屏風. 萬年大怒, 欲杖之, 曰: 乃公教戒汝, 汝反睡不聽吾言, 何也?

⁷⁷ 乃翁 is somewhat equivalent to 乃公. *Nai* 乃 is used in the sense of "your."

⁷⁸ *Chêng tzŭ t'ung: s. v. fu*, father.

⁷⁹ *I Ching*, 4.16a: 家人有嚴君焉, ⊙⊙之謂也. *Hsiao Ching* 聖治章, 5.1a: 孝莫大於嚴⊙.

⁸⁰ *Shih shuo hsin yü*, 1A.3a: 家君. Here the term *chia chün* is used both as a complimentary and depreciatory term. [From this point in Dr. Fêng's article the editors have been forced to revert to their usual practice of providing only indispensable citations from the Chinese.]

⁸¹ *Chin shu* 43.6b. *Chia kung* is no longer used in this sense; it is now used for mother's father.

The complimentary term is *tsun ta jen* 尊大人. *Tsun chün*,[82] *tsun kung*,[83] *tsun hou*,[84] *fêng wêng, fêng chün*,[85] in modern times are literary rather than vocative.

K'ao 考 is a posthumous term. In ancient literature it was also used for the living father, being synonymous with *fu*.[86] At present, however, it is primarily an epitaphic term. At different periods *k'ao* was used with various modifiers to express special circumstances. In the *Chü Li* of the *Li Chi*, *huang k'ao*[87] is used as a posthumous term for father, but in the *Chi Fa* of the same work it is used as a temple term for father's father's father.[88] *Wang k'ao* is a temple term in the *Li Chi* for father's father in connection with sacrifices,[89] but during the T'ang period it was occasionally used as a posthumous term for father.[90] *Huang k'ao* and *wang k'ao* have been prohibited for common use since the Yüan dynasty, being reserved only for the imperial family.[91] Thereafter the term *hsien k'ao* came into use as a universal epitaphic form.[92] But this term sharply contradicts the old usage, since in the *Li Chi*, *hsien k'ao* is used as a temple term for father's father's father's father.[93]

Fu chün 府君 is another popular epitaphic term. Originally, i. e., in the Han dynasty, only those who had been governors (*t'ai*

[82] *Shih shuo hsin yü*, 2A. 1a; *Chin shu*, 75. 5a. Sometimes *chün chia tsun* is used, e. g., *Shih Shuo hsin yü*, 2B. 34a.
[83] *Chin Shu*, 82. 1b; *ibid.*, 92. 23b.
[84] *Shih shuo hsin yü*, 1A. 28b: 尊侯.
[85] 封翁 and 封君 were used originally for those who received titles through sons who had risen to high official positions. Later they became common complimentary terms.
[86] According to the *Shuo Wên*, *k'ao* means "old." Thus it could be applied to any old man. Its application to mean father is a later development and its use as a posthumous term is a still later specialization. Cf. *Ch'in shu chi* 1. 5.
[87] *Li Chi*, 5. 22a.
[88] *Ibid.*, 46. 8b-9a: 皇考.
[89] *Ibid.* 46. 8-9: 王考.
[90] *Ch'ang-li chi* 24. 10a.
[91] This prohibition is best illustrated in the *Yüan tien chang* 元典章, 1908 edition, 31. 16a-b.
[92] The term *hsien k'ao* 顯考 was used for father much earlier than the Yüan period, e. g., *Shu Ching* (K'ang kao), 14. 3a. It continued to be used down to the fourth and fifth centuries A. D. for parents both living and dead. *Hsien* means "great," "illustrious," etc. Down to the Sung period, *hsien* is predominantly used in the posthumous sense. Cf. also the *Chin Shih Li*, 5. 55b.
[93] 鄭珍 [*Ch'in shu chi*, 2. 3a] rather bemoans such contradiction.

shou 太守) could be called *fu chün* by their sons, but since the T'ang period the term has been used indiscriminately.[94] The ordinary posthumous terms are *hsien fu* 先父, *wang fu* 亡父, *hsien ta fu* 先大夫, *hsien chün* 先君, *hsien tzŭ* 先子, *hsien chün tzŭ* 先君子,[95] *hsien kung* 先公,[96] etc. The complimentary posthumous terms are *tsun hsien chün* 尊先君 and *tsun fu* 尊府.[97]

The ancient temple term for father is *ni* 禰.[98]

34. Mu 母 mother

Mu, like *fu*, is primarily a standard term and is seldom used in the vocative. Other ancient alternative terms are *yü*[99] and *wên*,[100] but these terms can be applied to any old woman. During the T'ang period, *niang tzŭ*[101] was used for mother but at the same time it was also used for any young woman. This usage seemed to be northern. *Niang tzŭ* is used in modern terminology sometimes as a husband's term for wife, sometimes for any young woman.

The most peculiar variant of the term for mother is *tzŭ tzŭ* 姊姊 which was used by the royalty of the Northern Ch'i dynasty;[102] *tzŭ* being a term for older sister. According to the *Shuo Wên*, the people of Shu call mother *chieh* and the people of Huai nan call mother *shê*.[103] The older form of *chieh* 姐, according to the *Yü P'ien*, is written 毑. In the 説山訓 of the *Huai nan tzŭ*, *shê* is used for mother and Kao Yu comments that it is a Chiang Huai practice.[104] The *Shuo Wên* also states that *shih* 媞 was used

---

[94] Cf. *Hêng yen lu*, 3.3b-5b; *Ch'êng wei lu*, 1.21a-b.
[95] *Hsien chün* and *hsien tzŭ* originally were terms used during the feudal period by the nobility in referring to their deceased fathers. They became common terms at about the end of the period.
[96] *Hou Han Shu* 93.15a.   [97] *Ch'ang-li chi* 21.6b.
[98] *Tso Chuan* 32.4b. *Ni* means "near," "closer," i.e., the father is nearer than the father's father, etc. It is the same as 昵. Cf. also *Shu Ching* 10.11a.
[99] 嫗, *Shuo wên*; *Hsin Shu* 3.1b.
[100] 媼, *Shuo wên*; *Kuang ya*; *Han fei tzŭ* 10b. Also read *ao*.
[101] 娘子, *Shu* I, 1.9b-10a; for its uses during the various periods, cf. *Kai yü ts'ung kao*, 38.1a-3a.
[102] *Pei Ch'i shu* 9.4a.
[103] Hsü Shên seems to consider 社 a variant of 姐.
[104] *Huai nan tzŭ* 16.12a-b. Chiang Huai is the area between the Yangtze and Huai Rivers.

for mother in Chiang Huai. Kuo P'o (267-324 A. D.) said that the people of Chiang Tung [105] called mother *shih* 恀, also pronounced *chih*, or *ch'ih*. *Shê, shih, chih* and *ch'ih* all seem to have been derived from the same root and probably represent variants of *chieh*.[106] Apparently, from the third century B. C. to the fourth century A. D., *chieh*, with its variant forms, was a very prevalent vocative for mother throughout the Yangtze valley. Even down to the thirteenth century A. D. mother was sometimes called *chieh chieh*.[107] On the other hand, from Han to T'ang times *chia chia* was frequently used for mother and might be another variant transcription of *chieh chieh*.[108]

Perhaps due to the close similarity of these two sounds—*tzŭ* and *chieh*—and to the vagaries of transcription, for a time *tzŭ* was used for *chieh*. *Tzŭ*, being the older and more literary term, triumphed over *chieh*, and the latter lost its original meaning and acquired the meaning of older sister, like *tzŭ*. This seems the only reasonable explanation, and, if true, means that we have here an exact parallel with *hsiung* and *ko*, as discussed above. Apparently, no marital relations are involved.

The universal modern vocative is *ma* 媽 or *ma ma*.[109] *Niang* 娘,[110] or *niang niang*, are also very commonly used in many localities. The *Kuang Yün* says that the people of Ch'u called mother *ni*.[111] The *Chi Yün* states that the people of Ch'i called mother *mi*,[112] and the people of Wu called mother *mi*.[113] *Ni* and

---

[105] Chiang Tung is a vague geographical term, approximately the lower Yangtze delta.

[106] According to CHÊNG Chên (*Ch'in shu chi*, 1. 6b) the ancient pronunciation of *chieh* 姐 and 社 *shê* was about the same and both were in the rhymes 魚, 虞, 模 which are very close. Hence he considers *shê* to be a dialectical variant of *chieh*.

[107] *Ssŭ ch'ao wên chien lu* 四朝聞見錄, 已集, by YEH Shao-wêng 葉紹翁, ca, 1220 A. D. [知齋不足叢書 edition] 16a.

[108] *Pei Ch'i shu* 12. 8b: 家家.

[109] But cf. *Hsi shang fu t'an* 席上腐談, by Yü Yen 俞琰 [寶顏堂秘笈 edition] 1. 2a.

[110] As explained before, *niang* can be used in various designations sometimes overriding generations. Used as a vocative for mother, it was first noticed during the fourth and fifth centuries A. D. *Nan Shih* 44. 5a-b; *Pei Shih* 64. 13b-14a.

[111] 嬭; cf. *Ch'in shu chi*, 1. 6. Ch'u 楚 is the ancient term for the middle Yangtze valley and at present approximately the modern Hupeh and Hunan provinces.

[112] 彌安. Cf. also the *Yü p'ien*. Ch'i is the old name for the modern province of Shantung.

[113] 媄. Wu is the ancient name for roughly the southern part of Kiangsu province.

mi may be early dialectical variants of *ma*. The Miao, Yao and Tung tribes of Southwest China still call mother *mi* or *ma*.[114] Whether the aboriginal terms influenced the Chinese, or vice versa, or whether they both have been derived from a common earlier form, we at present have no way to determine. Certainly *ma* is only a slightly differing version of *mu*.[115]

Mu ch'in 母親 is sometimes used as a vocative, but more commonly in addressing one's mother in a letter; in the latter case, *ta jên* and *ch'i hsia* must be suffixed.

The depreciatory term is *chia mu*,[116] or *chia tz'ŭ*.[117] *Tz'ŭ* literally means "the affectionate one." *Tsun lao*[118] was used around the fifth century A. D., and *chia fu jên* was allowable during the Later Han times.[119]

Ling mu 令母,[120] *ling tz'ŭ* 令慈, *ling t'ang* 令堂, and *tsun t'ang* 尊堂,[121] are the most common complimentary terms. *Tsun shang*[122] and *tsun fu jên*[123] were used from the fifth to the eighth centuries A. D. At present *tsun fu jên* is used as a complimentary term for another's wife. *T'ai fu jên*[124] may be used for another's mother when the father is dead. *An jên* 安人 and *kung jên* 恭人, originally terms for a titled woman, may be used loosely, if incorrectly, as complimentary terms.

The posthumous term is *pi*,[125] as defined by the *Shuo Wên*. Yet this view is sometimes disputed, since in classical literature the term was often used indiscriminately for both living and dead

---

[114] *Miao fang pei lan, op. cit.*, 8. 6a, and 9. 10a. *Ling piao chi man, op. cit.*, 137.
[115] *Ch'in shu chi*, 1. 7a.
[116] *Yen shih chia hsün*, 2. 4b-5a. It seems that the prefixing of *chia* (house) to the terms of lineal ascendants to form depreciatory terms was not prevalent during Yen's time.
[117] This is the opposite of the term *chia yen*, "the stern one," for father. The mother is supposed to be affectionate and the father, stern.
[118] *Sung Shu* 91. 15a: 尊老.
[119] *Hou Han Shu* 78. 9a: 家夫人.
[120] *Ts'ai chung-lang chi* 6. 7b.
[121] *Lu shih-lung wên chi* 10. 10a. *T'ang* 堂 is derived from *pei t'ang* 北堂, a non-vocative, non-referential literary term for mother. Cf. *T'ung su pien*, 18. 5a-5b.
[122] *Sung shu* 91. 15a: 尊上.
[123] *Ch'ang-li chi* 29. 3b: 尊夫人.
[124] This was originally used for a titled woman, e. g., *Han Shu* 4. 12a-b: 太夫人.
[125] 妣. The *Êrh Ya* uses *mu* and *pi* synonymously.

mother. The modern usage follows the interpretation of the *Li Chi*, that *mu* is used when the mother is living, and *pi* when she is dead.¹²⁶ *Huang pi*¹²⁷ was an old sacrificial term but has been forbidden since the Yüan period. *Hsien pi*¹²⁸ is exclusively an epitaphic term.

35. Po fu 伯父 f o b

The old term in the *Êrh Ya* and *I Li* is *shih fu*.¹²⁹ In the *Li Chi*, *po fu*¹³⁰ is sometimes used in place of *shih fu*. *Po* itself means oldest, e. g., an oldest brother may be called *po hsiung*, and an oldest sister, *po tzŭ*. Since the Wei and Chin periods, *po* alone has been used as a vocative for father's older brother.¹³¹ From the Sung period down to modern times, *po po* has been the most prevalent vocative. The posthumous term is *wang po* 亡伯. *Ts'ung hsiung ti mên chung*¹³² is an old term used *circa* the fifth century A. D. but seldom heard today.

36. Po mu 伯母 f o b w

Shih mu is the old term used in the *Êrh Ya*, *I Li*¹³³ and *Li Chi*.¹³⁴ *Po mu* is also used in the *Li Chi*.¹³⁵

37. Shu fu 叔父 f y b

Circa the latter half of the first millennium B. C., *chu fu*,¹³⁶ *ts'ung fu*,¹³⁷ and *yu fu*¹³⁸ were used for father's brothers, both

---

¹²⁶ *Li Chi* 5. 22b.　　　　　　　¹²⁷ *Ibid.* 5. 22a.
¹²⁸ *Wang shih chung chi* 38a: 顯⊙ This is, perhaps, the first use of *hsien pi*, but it is used for the living mother. Now *hsien pi* is used exclusively as a corresponding term to *hsien k'ao*.
¹²⁹ *I Li* 30. 8b. *Shih* means "generation." That is, the father's older brother is the one in the father's "generation" to succeed to the grandfather.
¹³⁰ *Li Chi* 18. 10a: 伯.
¹³¹ See p. 197, note 89.
¹³² *Yen shih chia hsün* 2. 6a: 從兄弟門中. It literally means "within the gate of father's brother's sons," a circumlocution for expressing a mournful situation.
¹³³ *I Li* 30. 9b-10a.
¹³⁴ *Li Chi* 18. 15a.
¹³⁵ *Ibid.*, 43. 2b.
¹³⁶ *Shih Ching* 9C. 2a: 諸⊙. *Chu fu* is a very vague term, literally "the fathers."
¹³⁷ *I Li* 31. 17a: 從⊙昆弟. Since father's brother's sons can be called *ts'ung fu k'un ti*, father's brothers can be called *ts'ung fu*. *Pei shih* 22. 8.
¹³⁸ *Li Chi* 8. 4b-5a: 猶⊙. Since brother's sons can be called *yu tzŭ*, it is inferred that father's brother can be called *yu fu*, "like father."

older and younger. They are still used today as alternative terms but are primarily literary forms. *Ts'ung fu*, a contraction of *ts'ung tsu fu*, was also used for father's father's brother's sons.

Shu fu also was used in another sense in early times. The father's first younger brother was called *chung fu*, the second younger brother, *shu fu*, and the youngest, *chi fu*.[139] This usage was never common. *Chi fu* was also used for father's younger brothers in general, not necessarily his youngest brother.[140] *Ts'ung wêng* is a relatively late and uncommon term.[141]

Since the third century A. D. *shu, a shu,* or *shu shu* have been used as common vocatives.

Among the royal families of the Northern Ch'i and T'ang dynasties, father's brothers were called *a hsiung*; this may be a family peculiarity.

The depreciatory term is *chia shu fu*, or simply *chia shu*. Yen's *Family Instructions* states that it is incorrect to use *chia po* for father's older brother, since he is an elder of father and one dare not use *chia*.[142] This is somewhat over-rationalistic; *chia po* is the most common form today. The complimentary term for another's father's younger brother is *hsien shu*, or *ling shu*.

The posthumous term is *wang shu*. *Ts'ung hsiung ti mên chung* is an old term both for father's older and younger brothers.

38. Shu mu 叔母 f y b w

This is also the term used in the *Êrh Ya*. *Chi mu*[143] was used during the Han period, but rarely. The vocative *shên*[144] dates from the Sung dynasty. This term is not found in the classical literature, and is thought to be a contraction of *shih mu*. In modern times *shên shên, shên mu,* or *shên niang* have been commonly used as vocatives. Another common usage is by prefixing her sib-name, or the numerical order of her husband, to *ma*. This also applies to 36.

[139] *Shih Ming*: 季⊙.
[140] *Shih chi* 7.1b; *Ch'ang-li Chi* 23.9b; Han Yü refers to himself as *chi fu*.
[141] *T'ang chih yen*, 3.1a: 從翁.
[142] *Yen shih chia hsün* 2.5a.
[143] *Hou Han Shu* 118.20a.
[144] *Ming tao tsa chih*, 13b: 嬸.

39. Ku mu 姑母 f si

"Father's sisters are ku," defines the *Êrh Ya*. *Ku* is also used in the *I Li*.[145]

The vocative for father's unmarried sister is *ku*, or *ku ku* prefixed by her name or numerical order. When she is married, *ku ma* is the most prevalent form.

Chia ku mu is sometimes used as a depreciatory term. Yen's *Family Instructions* considered this usage incorrect, for when a woman was married out she was no longer a member of the family, so that *chia* could not be applied.[146]

40. Ku fu 姑父 f si h

Ku hsü[147] and *ku fu*[148] are used as alternative terms, mostly from the third to the sixth centuries A. D.

41. T'ang po fu 堂伯父 f f b s > f

Êrh Ya gives the term *ts'ung tsu fu* for father's father's brother's sons, both older and younger than father. By inference from other usages, *ts'ung tsu shih fu* may be used for the former. Since the Han period, *ts'ung po*, or *ts'ung po fu* have been used.[149] During the fifth and sixth centuries A. D. the term *t'ung t'ang* was introduced, since agnate relatives of the same paternal grandfather offer sacrifices in the same ancestral hall. *T'ung t'ang* literally means "the same hall." During the T'ang period the *t'ung* was dropped and only *t'ang* was used.[150] Later the term was extended to other collateral lines.

42. T'ang po mu 堂伯母 w of 41

As can be inferred from *ts'ung tsu fu* and *ts'ung tsu shih fu*, the older term would be *ts'ung tsu mu* or *ts'ung tsu shih mu*.

---

[145] *I Li* 31.16b-17a. LIANG Ch'ang-chü (*Chêng wei lu*, 8.13a-14b) considers *ku tzŭ mei* a term for father's sister. As far as its use in the *I Li* is concerned, it should be interpreted as *ku* (father's sister), and *tzŭ* and *mei* (ego's own sisters). The other instances which Liang cites in support of the use of *ku tzŭ* for father's older sister, and *ku mei* for father's younger sister, are very questionable.

[146] *Yen shih chia hsün* 2.5a.
[147] *Pei Ch'i Shu* 18.3b: 婿.
[148] *San Kuo Chih* 13.3a; *Nan Shih* 57.14a.
[149] *Chin Shu* 80.1a.   [150] CH'IEN Ta-hsin [*Hêng yen lu*, 3.9a-b].

Since the Han period *ts'ung po mu* or simply *ts'ung mu* have been used.

43. T'ang shu fu 堂叔父 f f b s ⟨ f

Compare 41. *Ts'ung tsu shu fu* may, by inference, be the older term. Since the Han period *ts'ung shu* or *ts'ung shu fu* [151] have been used as alternative terms.

In the vocatives of 41 and 43 the modifier *t'ang* is usually dropped, i. e., the vocatives of 35 and 37 may be applied here, respectively, modified by their names or numerical order.

44. T'ang shu mu 堂叔母 w of 43

Ts'ung tsu shu mu may be the older form. The later abbreviated form *ts'ung shu mu* may be used alternatively with *t'ang shu mu*. *T'ang shên* is a vocative extension of *shên*.

45. T'ang ku mu 堂姑母 f f b d

The term in the *Êrh Ya* is *ts'ung tsu ku*, later abbreviated to *ts'ung ku*.[152] *Ts'ung* and *t'ang* are synonymous. The vocative for father's sister may be used here, modified by her name or numerical order.

46. T'ang ku fu 堂姑父 f f b d h

The vocative for father's sister's husband may be used here, modified by his sibname.

47. Tsai ts'ung po fu 再從伯父 s of 25 or 27 ⟩ f

Tsu fu is the term used in the *Êrh Ya* and *I Li*.[153] *Tsu po fu* may be used for this relation, but it can be applied to any male sib relative of the father's generation older than father, from the fourth collateral line onward—so it is a rather loose term.

48. Tsai ts'ung po mu 再從伯母 w of 47

49. Tsai ts'ung shu fu 再從叔父 s of 25 or 27 ⟨ f

Tsu fu is used in the *Êrh Ya*. *Tsu shu* [154] and *tsung shu* [155] are later alternatives, but used rather loosely. In the vocatives of 47

---

[151] *Sung Shu* 52. 5a.
[152] *Chin Shu* 51. 2b.
[153] *I Li* 33. 6a: 族.
[154] *Chin Shu* 83. 1a.
[155] *Yin hua lu*, 2. 2a: 宗叔.

and 49, *tsai ts'ung* is usually dropped, leaving only *po* and *shu* modified by their names or numerical order.

50. Tsai ts'ung shu mu 再從叔母 w of 49.

The vocatives of 36 and 38 may be applied to 48 and 50, respectively, modified by their sibnames or their husbands' numerical order, or by both.

51. Tsai ts'ung ku mu 再從姑母 d of 25 or 27

In the *Êrh Ya, tsu tsu ku* 族祖姑. In modern times, *tsu ku* 族姑 has been used alternatively, but in a rather loose fashion.

52. Tsai ts'ung ku fu 再從姑父 h of 51

53. Ku piao po fu 姑表伯父 f f si s > f

Chung wai chang jên[156] was used during the fifth and sixth centuries A.D. During the Sung dynasty *piao chang jên*[157] and *wai po fu*[158] were frequently used. Before the T'ang period, *chang jên* was used as a polite term for any old man; but since then it has been used as a synonym for *yo fu*, wife's father.

54. Ku piao po mu 姑表伯母 w of 53

Chang mu[159] was used during the fifth and sixth centuries A.D., but is now used exclusively for wife's mother.

55. Ku piao shu fu   姑表叔父   f f si s < f

56. Ku piao shu mu   ○○叔母   w of 55

57. Ku piao ku mu   ○○姑母   f f si d

58. Ku piao ku fu   ○○姑父   f f si d h

59. Chiu piao po fu   舅表伯父   f m b s < f

60. Chiu piao po mu ○○伯母   w of 59

---

[156] 中外丈人, cf. *Yen shih chia hsün* 2.8b. *Chung-wai* is synonymous with *chung-piao*.

[157] *T'ai p'ing kuang chi* 太平廣記 [1934, Peiping, 文友堂 ed.] 148.4a.

[158] Cf. 東觀餘論附錄 [學津討原 ed.] 5a.

[159] *Yen Shih Chia hsün* 2.8b. The use of *wang* 王 *mu* and *hsieh* 謝 *mu* is no longer intelligible. Perhaps their use is based on the most well-known sibnames of the time, Wang and Hsieh.

61. Chiu piao shu fu 舅表叔父 f m b s < f
62. Chiu piao shu mu ○○叔母 w of 61
63. Chiu piao ku mu ○○姑母 f m b d
64. Chiu piao ku fu ○○姑父 h of 63
65. I piao po fu 姨表伯父 f m si s > f
66. I piao po mu ○○伯母 w of 65
67. I piao shu fu ○○叔父 f m si s < f
68. I piao shu mu ○○叔母 h of 67
69. I piao ku mu ○○姑母 f m si d
70. I piao ku fu ○○姑父 w of 69

The terms listed under 53 are applicable to 55, 58, 59, 61, 64, 65, 67 and 70 respectively, during the period mentioned above. In ordinary modern usage the modifiers *ku*, *chiu* and *i* are usually omitted, so that terminologically these relatives are not distinguished from one another. Conceptually, the exact relationship is always assumed.

V. Generation of the speaker

71. Pên shên 本身 ego, a male.

A female would use the same terms, except for those provided in Table IV and certain terms in Table III.

72. Ch'i 妻 wife

Ch'i tzŭ [160] 妻子 is commonly used, but it may also mean " wife and children." In certain cases *fu* [161] is used synonymously with *ch'i*, but it may be used to mean " woman " in general. In kinship usage *fu* is principally used for the wives of those who are of lower generations and age status.

[160] *Jih Chih lu*, 24. 5a.
[161] *I Ching*, 1. 33a: 婦.

Fei[162] is a very old term and so also is *nei chu*,[163] but the latter is rather uncommon. *Nei shê*[164] and *ju jên*[165] were commonly employed during the first half of the first millennium A. D. *Shih*,[166] *chia*,[167] and *shih chia*[168] are also very old terms, but are still commonly employed as literary forms.

Chieh fa[169] and *chung k'uei*[170] are primarily literary terms. *Chieh fa* is applied only to the first marriage principal wife; *chung k'uei* is also used as a literary complimentary term.

The wife, when speaking to the husband, calls herself *ch'ieh* 妾, " your concubine "; or, *chi chou ch'ieh*.[171] These abject terms are seldom, if ever, used except in literature. During the feudal period, a noble woman could on formal occasions, call herself *pei tzǔ*,[172] or *hsiao tung*,[173] according to rank. These terms are now entirely obsolete. *Chün fu*[174] is a common form, but mostly used in poetry.

The husband calls the wife *hsien ch'i*,[175] or *niang tzǔ*,[176] and, more anciently, *hsi chün*.[177] These highly complimentary terms are rarely used in daily life, and are rather mere literary forms. *Ch'ing* is a reciprocal term, i. e., used alike both by husband and

---

[162] 妃 *Êrh Ya*; *Shuo Wên*; *Shih Ming*. *Tso chuan* 5.19a; *Chan kuo ts'ê* 3.83a. *Fei*, as used before the Han period, is a term for " wife " in general. It is only during the Han period and since that *fei* is reserved for the wives of nobility and the Emperor's secondary wives. Cf. *Ch'in shu chi*, 2.5b-6b.

[163] *Tso Chuan* 42.9b: 內主. *Nei chu* literally means " inside lord."

[164] 琳陳:飲馬長城窟行 [*Yü t'ai hsin yung chi*, 1.13a]: 內舍.

[165] *Chiang Wên-t'ung chih* 1.1b: 孺人. *Ju jên* was originally a term for titled women during the feudal period, e. g., *Li Chi* 5.11b. It became a common term for wife during the third and fourth centuries A. D. Since then, it has reverted to its old connotation.

[166] *I Li* 6.8b: 室. *Li Chi* 28.20b.

[167] *Shih Ching* 7B.5b: 樂子之無家. *Tso chuan* 14.10b.

[168] *Shih Ching* 4A.6b: 室家.

[169] *Wên Hsüan*, 29.14b: 結髮.

[170] *I Ching* 4.17a: 中饋. *Chung k'uei* literally means " the family larder " and is used metaphorically.

[171] *Shih Chi* 8.4a: 箕帚妾; i. e., a female with broom and dust-basket ready to serve.

[172] *Tso Chuan* 15.2a: 婢子.

[173] *Lun Yü*, 16.10a: 小童; *Li Chi* 5.12a.

[174] *Shih Ching* 13B.6a: 君婦.

[175] 賢妻 literally " virtuous wife."

[176] *Pei Ch'i Shu* 39.5a: 娘子.

[177] *Han Shu* 65.5a: 細君.

wife, and is now a predominately literary form of address. Husband and wife may call each other by name, or they may use no term at all and just refer to each other as " you," " he," and " she." After issue, teknonymy is the most common practice.

The depreciatory term is *nei*.[178] *Nei tzŭ* 內子, *nei jên* 內人 and *pi nei* 敝內 are its derivatives. *Cho ching* [179] and *shih jên* [180] are more literary. The above terms are used mostly in refined society. *Chia li* [181] and *hsiang li* [182] are vulgar terms. *Hun chia*,[183] *hun shê*,[184] *lao p'o*,[185] and *chia chu p'o* [186] are vulgar and dialectical forms used mostly in the referential, and are not necessarily depreciatory.

The complimentary term is *fu jên* 夫人, originally a term for the wife of a man of rank. More intimately, *sao fu jên* 嫂夫人 may be used. *T'ai t'ai* is more colloquial.[187] *Ling shih* [188] and *ling ch'i* [189] are literary in nature. In ancient times *nei tzŭ* [190] was used as a complimentary term, but is now exclusively used as a

---

[178] It is also a general term used for wife and concubine together, e. g., *Tso Chuan* 14. 18b. Cf. *Hêng yen lu*, 3. 9b-10a and *Ch'êng wei lu*, 5. 12b-13b.

[179] 拙荊 is derived from the 荊釵布裙 of Mêng Kuang 孟光, wife of Liang Hung 梁鴻 of the Later Han dynasty. The variants are *shan ching* 山荊, *ching fu* 荊婦 and *ching jên* 荊人.

[180] *Shih Ching* 2C. 6a: 室人.

[181] " In the home." Cf. Yao K'uan 姚寬 ?-1161 A. D., 西溪叢話, 學津討原 ed., 2. 19b.

[182] 鄉里, " in the country." *Nan Shih* 64. 16a: 謂妻楊, 呼爲鄉里, 曰: 我不忍令鄉里落佗處, 今當先殺鄉里.

[183] *Nan T'ang chin shih* 南唐近事 of Chêng Wên-pao 鄭文寶, 953-1013 A. D. [寶顏堂祕笈 ed.] 3a-4b: 渾家; also Liang ch'i i kao 梁谿遺稿, 詩鈔 of Yu Mou 尤袤 1127-1194 A. D., [錫山尤氏叢刊 ed.] 淮民謠, 11b.

[184] 渾舍 is a variant of *hun-chia*.

[185] 老婆 " old woman." Cf. *Ch'êng wei lu*, 5. 10a. This is the most common modern term.

[186] *Hêng yen lu*, 3. 13b-14a: 家主婆.

[187] Ho Liang-chün 何良俊, *Ssŭ yu chai ts'ung shuo* 四友齋叢說 [紀錄彙編 ed.] 6. 52b-53a: 太太. Cf. also *T'ung su pien*, 18. 8a. During the Ming period, *t'ai t'ai* was a term for the wives of officials of the 中丞 rank and higher.

[188] 令室.

[189] *Shih Ching* 20B, 8b: 令妻.

[190] *Yen tzŭ ch'un ch'iu*, 6. 9a: 內子. *Nei tzŭ* was used during the feudal period as a term for the wife of ministers of the feudal lords, e. g., *Li Chi* 44. 16a, and *Shih ming*. Hence it is sometimes used as a complimentary term.

depreciatory term. *K'ang li*¹⁹¹ is a literary form used to refer to another's wife, and, more commonly, to refer to both husband and wife as *hsien kang li*.

*Pin*¹⁹² and *ling jên*¹⁹³ are posthumous terms for wife. *Tê pei*¹⁹⁴ is a posthumous complimentary term. It is also used as a literary form for the wife in the case of an aged couple.

73. Hsiung 兄 o b

The *Êrh Ya* used *hsiung* to explain *k'un*.¹⁹⁵ The two terms apparently were synonymous in ancient times. Kuo P'o's (276-324 A.D.) commentary on the *Êrh Ya* states that the people of Chiang Tung called older brother *k'un*. The *Shuo Wên* does not give the character 兄, but gives the character 㷊, and states that the Chou people used this term for older brother. 㷊 is probably its original form and 㷊 and 弟, its variants. 昆 is a later borrowed form.¹⁹⁶ In the *Shih Ching*, only the *Wang Fêng* (4A. 9a) uses the term *k'un*, all others using *hsiung*. This fact is regarded as evidence that *k'un* is a Chou term.

In the *I Li* all male paternal cousins of the same sibname of ego and within the *Ta Kung* degree of mourning are given as *k'un ti*, and all male paternal cousins of the same sibname but beyond the *Ta Kung* degree of mourning, and all male cousins of different sibnames from ego are given as *hsiung ti*.¹⁹⁷ This illustrates the intentional differentiation and standardization of the degrees of relationship adopted by the ritual books in employing terms in other than their original connotation. *K'un* is entirely obsolete at present.¹⁹⁸

¹⁹¹ *Tso Chuan* 27. 2b: 伉儷.   ¹⁹² *Li Chi* 5. 22b: 嬪.
¹⁹³ *Chu tzŭ nien p'u* 朱子年譜 by Wang Mu-hung 王懋竑 1668-1764 A.D. 【粵雅堂叢書本】 2A. 13a: 令人.
¹⁹⁴ *Ch'êng wei lu*, 5. 14a: 德配.
¹⁹⁵ *Êrh Ya*: 㷊.
¹⁹⁶ The *Shuo wên* lists the character 㷊 but not with the meaning "older brother." The *Yü p'ien* gives 㷊 and states that it is the same as 昆. Huang K'an 皇侃 [488-545 A.D.] says, that *k'un* 昆 means "bright," "brilliant." Out of reverence the older brother is called *k'un* (論語義疏, 6. 2b-3a, 古經解彙函 edition). This is rather a rationalization.
¹⁹⁷ *Ch'êng wei lu*, 4. 2b.
¹⁹⁸ For a most complete and classical study of the difference between these characters, cf. 昆弟兄弟釋異 by Tsang Yung 臧庸, 1767-1811, 拜經堂文集 [1930], 1.

The vocative is *ko*¹⁹⁹ 哥 or *ko ko* a euphonic duplication. *Ko*, as given in the *Shuo Wên*, does not mean older brother at all; it means " to sing," or " a song." *Ko* was first used from the sixth to the eighth centuries A. D., to mean father and then in the ninth and tenth centuries A. D. it became a vocative for older brother.²⁰⁰

According to the *Fang Yên*, the people of Chin and Yang called older brother *po* or *p'o*.²⁰¹ The *Shih Ming* says that the people of Ch'ing and Hsü used the term *huang* 荒. Until the fourteenth to the seventeenth centuries A. D. the peoples of the lower Yangtze delta still called older brother 況 *huang*.²⁰² 況 and 荒 are pronounced about the same. The ancient pronunciation of *hsiung* 兄 may have been *huang* 況, as the two characters are often used interchangeably.²⁰³ The *Pai hu t'ung* uses 況 to explain 兄.

74. Sao 嫂 o b w

The *Êrh Ya* reads, " Woman calls older brother's wife *sao*," but it does not give the man's term. Whether or not *sao* was exclusively a woman's term we have no means of knowing. The *Shuo Wên* defines *sao* as " older brother's wife " but does not specify man or woman; it was most probably a term for both man and woman.²⁰⁴

75. Ti 弟 y b

The younger brother, when speaking to the older brother or sister, calls himself *pi ti*,²⁰⁵ or *hsiao ti*.²⁰⁶ The older brother or sister calls the younger brother *hsien ti*.²⁰⁷ These were old usages; at present simply *ti* is used.

---

¹⁹⁹ *Kuang yün*.
²⁰⁰ *Kai yü ts'ung k'ao*, 37. 25b.
²⁰¹ *Fang Yen*, 10. 4a: 䏳 Its pronunciation is very uncertain.
²⁰² *Yen pei tsa chih* 研北雜志, by Lu Yu 陸友, ca. 1330 A. D. [得月簃 edition] 49a.
²⁰³ *Shih Ching*, 3A. 7a; *ibid.*, 18B. 1a; *Han shu*, 76. 6a, with YEN Shih-ku's note.
²⁰⁴ For example, *Chan kuo ts'ê* 3. 6a.
²⁰⁵ *San kuo chih* 29. 26a (commentary): 鄙弟.
²⁰⁶ 木蘭詩: 小弟.
²⁰⁷ *Shih Chi* 86. 9a: 賢弟.

Chia ti [208] was used as a depreciative from the third to the eighth centuries A. D. It is now incorrect to use this term. The present term is *shê ti*, and the complimentary term, *ling ti* or *hsien ti*.

76. Ti fu 弟婦 y b w

Ti hsi 弟媳 is an alternative term. *Fu* and *hsi* are synonymous in relationship terminology. The older brother usually avoids the younger brother's wife, and vice versa. Conversation can be only formal, and a proper distance must be maintained.

77. Tzŭ 姊 o si

Tzŭ is now used chiefly in standard and literary contexts. It may be doubled as *tzŭ tzŭ*. The universal vocative is *chieh* or *chieh chieh*. Compare 34 for changes of *chieh*. *Chieh* may also be used for any young woman, e. g., *hsiao chieh*, which is equivalent to " Miss."

Hsü [209] was an ancient term for older sister, used in the state of Ch'u; *shao* [210] was used in Ch'i. *Mêng* [211] was an old term for father's concubine's daughter older than father's principal wife's daughter. Later, in certain regions, it was used to mean older sister in general.[212] *Nü hsiung* [213] may be used as a literary alternative for *tzŭ*.

78. Tzŭ fu 姊夫 o si h

The term in the *Êrh Ya* is *shêng*—a reflection of cross-cousin marriage. *Tzŭ chang* and *tzŭ hsü* [214] are modern alternatives. *Chieh fu* is nore colloquial. Teknonymy is the most common practice as regards the vocative. If there is no child, brother terms are usually used.

The *Êrh Ya* says that sisters call each other's husband *ssŭ*,[215] " private "; this is considered evidence of the sororate. It has

---

[208] *Ts'ao tzŭ ch'ien chi* 釋思賦序, 1. 5b; *T'ang shu* 162. 22b.

[209] *Li Sao* [*Wên Hsüan*, 32. 9b]: 嬃; also *Shuo Wên*.

[210] *Kuang yün*: 穮.

[211] *Tso chuan* 2. 2a: 孟.

[212] *Fang yen*, 12. 1a.   [213] *Shuo wên*: 女兄.

[214] *Hou Han Shu* 49. 12b: ⊙; *Chin Shu* 39. 8a-b. [No. 18 on p. 150.]

[215] 私. *Shih Ching* 3B. 9a. The *Shih ming* gives the traditional, but rationalistic, explanation.

long been obsolete. In modern times, brother and sister use the same term.

79. Mei 妹 y si

*Ti*²¹⁶ is said to be a woman's term for younger sister but this is by no means certain. During the feudal period *ti* had a special connotation in connection with the *yin* marriage. *Nü ti*²¹⁷ is a literary alternative term for *mei*. The *Shuo Wên* states that the people of Ch'u called younger sister *wei*,²¹⁸ which may be a variant of *mei*.

The depreciatory term *chia tzǔ* is used for older sister, and *shê mei* for younger sister. This use of these terms is continued even after the sisters are married, although theoretically this should not be done.

80. Mei fu 妹夫 y si h

In the *Êrh Ya* the term is *shêng*—a reflection of cross-cousin marriage. The *Êrh Ya* also says that sisters call one another's husbands *ssǔ*—a supposed reflection of the sororate. *Mei chang* and *mei hsü* are modern alternatives. For other usages, compare 78.

81. T'ang hsiung 堂兄 f b s > e

Ts'ung fu k'un ti is the term in the *Êrh Ya* and *I Li* ²¹⁹ for the first male paternal cousins. Later it was abbreviated to *ts'ung hsiung* ²²⁰ for the father's brother's sons older than speaker, and *ts'ung ti* ²²¹ for those younger than the speaker. *Kung k'un ti* was used in the *Shih Chi*.²²² During the fifth and sixth centuries A. D. *t'ung t'ang* was substituted for *ts'ung*, e. g., *t'ung t'ang hsiung* and *t'ung t'ang ti*. During the latter part of the T'ang

---

²¹⁶ *Shih Ming*: 娣. This interpretation is followed by CHÊNG Chên in his *Ch'ao ching ch'ao wên chi,* 1.17b-18a. This view is hardly justifiable, however, on the basis of the *Êrh Ya*'s use of *mei* and *ti*. The former is used both by man and woman; the latter, in reference to the *yin* custom of the feudal period, refers to younger sisters who have married the same man. Thus *ti* can also be applied to husband's younger brother's wife, as in the *Êrh Ya*.
²¹⁷ *Shuo wên*: 女弟.
²¹⁸ 娟. Cf. also *Kung-yang chuan* 4. 7b.
²¹⁹ *I Li* 31. 17a.   ²²¹ *San kuo chih* 8. 1a.
²²⁰ *Liang Shu* 31. 1a.   ²²² *Shih Chi* 49. 6a: 公.

dynasty the *t'ung* was dropped, only *t'ang hsiung* and *t'ang ti* being used. *T'ang* and *ts'ung* can still be used alternatively.

82. T'ang sao 堂嫂 w of 81

83. T'ang ti 堂弟 f b s < e

84. T'ang ti fu 堂弟婦 w of 83

85. T'ang tzŭ 堂姊 f b d > e

The older term is *ts'ung fu tzŭ mei* for father's brother's daughters, both older and younger than speaker. The development is exactly parallel with that of 81, *t'ang hsiung*.

86. T'ang tzŭ fu ○○夫 h of 85

87. T'ang mei 堂妹 f b d < e

88. T'ang mei fu ○○夫 h of 87

89. Tsai ts'ung hsiung 再從兄 f f b s s > e

The older term is *ts'ung tsu k'un ti*, as used in the *Êrh Ya* and the *I Li*.[223] *Tsai ts'ung* was substituted later. *Tsai* means "once again" or "a second time." *Ts'ung* is synonymous with the later term *t'ang*, which indicates the second collateral line. Hence *tsai ts'ung* indicated the third collateral line.

90. Tsai ts'ung sao 再從嫂 w of 89

91. Tsai ts'ung ti 再從弟 f f b s s < e

92. Tsai ts'ung ti fu 再從弟婦 w of 91

93. Tsai ts'ung tzŭ 再從姊 f f b s d > e

94. Tsai ts'ung tzŭ fu 再從姊夫 h of 93

95. Tsai ts'ung mei 再從妹 f f b s d < e

96. Tsai ts'ung mei fu 再從妹夫 h of 95

97. Tsu hsiung 族兄 f f f b s s s > e

The alternative and more exact term is *san ts'ung hsiung* 三從

[223] *I Li* 33.1b: 祖.

兄. San means "third," and ts'ung signifies second collateral. Hence san ts'ung means the fourth collateral line, since ts'ung begins the count from the second collateral line. This principle can be extended and the terms formed, e. g., ssŭ ts'ung, wu ts'ung, liu ts'ung, indicating the fifth, sixth, seventh collateral lines, respectively. Tsu 族 is a vague term applied to all sib relatives from the fourth collateral line and beyond, without further discrimination. Tsung hsiung [224] is a modern alternative. Tsung 宗 is in a certain sense synonymous with tsu 族. Ts'ung tsêng tsu k'un ti [225] was used during the Han period; it is a rather clumsy device involving the enumeration of ancestors.

Ch'in t'ung hsing [226] is the term given in the Êrh Ya for male paternal cousins of the same sibname, of the fifth collateral line. It is obsolete now; generally tsu hsiung ti is used, or, more exactly, ssŭ ts'ung hsiung ti.

98. Tsu sao 族嫂 w of 97

99. Tsu ti 族弟 f f f b s s s < e

100. Tsu ti fu 族弟婦 w of 99

101. Tsu tzŭ 族姊 f f f b s s d > e

102. Tsu tzŭ fu 族姊夫 h of 101

103. Tsu mei 族妹 f f f b s s d < e

104. Tsu mei fu 族妹夫 h of 103

The vocatives for brothers and sisters, brothers' wives and sisters' husbands can be correspondingly applied to 81-104, individualized by their names, numerical order, or sibnames. Depreciatory and complimentary forms can be formed in the regular way.

105. Ku piao hsiung 姑表兄 f si s > e

The old term in the Êrh Ya is shêng—a reflection of cross-

---

[224] 宗兄 is just as indefinite as tsu hsiung, and can be applied to any older sib-brother from the fourth collateral line and beyond. But tsung hsiung was used during the feudal period by younger brothers to refer to the primogenitary eldest brother. Li Chi 19.10b-11a.

[225] Hsin Shu 8.6a-b.   [226] 親同姓.

cousin marriage. During the Han period *wai hsiung ti*[227] and *ts'ung nei hsiung ti*[228] were used for both the older and the younger. The term *piao* also dates from this period. *Shêng, wai hsiung ti* and *ts'ung nei hsiung ti* are all obsolete now.

In the vocative *ku* is always dropped, leaving only *piao hsiung* or *piao ko*. *Piao hsiung* is more literary and formal, *piao ko* is strictly vocative. In certain localities *lao piao* 老表 is used.

106. Ku piao sao 姑表嫂 w of 105
 Vocative *piao sao*.
107. Ku piao ti 姑表弟 f si s ⟨ e
108. Ku piao ti fu ○○弟婦 w of 107
109. Ku piao tzŭ ○○姊 f si d ⟨ e
 Vocative *piao chieh*.
110. Ku piao tzŭ fu ○○姊夫 h of 109
111. Ku piao mei ○○妹 f si d ⟨ e
112. Ku piao mei fu ○○妹夫 h of 111
113. T'ang ku piao hsiung 堂姑表兄 f f si s ⟩ e
114. T'ang ku piao sao ○○表嫂 w of 113
115. T'ang ku piao ti ○○表弟 f f si s ⟨ e
116. T'ang ku piao ti fu ○○○弟婦 w of 115
117. T'ang ku piao tzŭ ○○○姊 f f si s d ⟩ e
118. T'ang ku piao tzŭ fu ○○○姊夫 h of 117
119. T'ang ku piao mei ○○○妹 f f si s d ⟨ e
120. T'ang ku piao mei fu ○○○妹夫 h of 119

Terms 113-120 may also be applied to the children of father's father's brother's daughter. This is by inference only; no documentary usage has been noted.

[227] *I Li* 33. 9b.   [228] *Wên Hsüan*, 25. 1a.

VI. Generation of the son

121. Tzŭ 子 son

Tzŭ, in ancient times, was used to mean child, either male or female. Thus it was often compounded with other elements to signify son, e. g., *chang fu tzŭ*.²²⁹ *Êrh* ²³⁰ is synonymous with *tzŭ*; it is now used mostly as a diminutive, with no sex connotation, so that it has to be combined with other elements to express son, as in the modern term *êrh tzŭ*.²³¹ *Hsi* ²³² is an old term for son, but also has the indefinite meaning of child; consequently, the forms *hsi nan* ²³³ for son and *hsi nü* for daughters are used. *Ssŭ* 嗣 ²³⁴ means " descendant," and is also used for son. During the feudal period *ssŭ tzŭ* ²³⁵ referred to the eldest succeeding son, but in modern terminology is used for the adopted son. *Hsing*,²³⁶ in ancient times, may be used for son but it may mean any descendant, being synonymous with *shêng*,²³⁷ " to bear." *Nu* ²³⁸ is another old term.

Ku and *ni* ²³⁹ were uncommon old, perhaps local, terms for son. *Tsai* 崽 ²⁴⁰ and *tsai* 囝 ²⁴¹ are modern dialectical forms, apparently derivatives from *tzŭ*. 囝 may also be pronounced *chien*.²⁴²

Tzŭ can be combined with various modifiers to express the more

---

²²⁹ *Shih Chi* 67. 19a-b: 夫子丈; literally, " male child."
²³⁰ *Kuang ya*: 兒.
²³¹ *Shih Chi* 52. 2a.
²³² 息 means " to reproduce," or " to bear." Hence it is used both for male and female children. See note 233, and p. 239, note 255.
²³³ *Ts'ao tzŭ-chien chi* 8. 1.
²³⁴ *Shu Ching* 4. 7a.
²³⁵ *Li Chi* 4. 5a.
²³⁶ *Shih Ching* 1C. 7a: 姓; and *Tso Chuan* 42. 32a.
²³⁷ Since the ancient pronunciation of *hsing* is about the same as 生, they are used interchangeably. *Shih Ching* 20D. 7b.
²³⁸ *Shih Ching* 9B. 10b: 帑.
²³⁹ *Kuang Ya*: 縠, 倪. Cf. 王念孫, 廣雅疏證, 6B. 4.
²⁴⁰ *Fang Yen*, 10. 1b.
²⁴¹ *Chêng tzŭ t'ung*, *s. v.*
²⁴² CHÊNG Chên (*Ch'in shu chi*, 2. 12b) says that the *Chi Yün* gives the pronunciation 九件切. This is incorrect and probably a confusion with 夯. But *chien* may be a T'ang pronunciation, e. g., in *Hua yang chi*, 1. 13a. However, at present the character is pronounced differently in different localities. In Fukien, it is pronounced " chan," in Chekiang and Kiangsu, " lan," and in Kiangsi, Kwangtung, Hupeh and Hunan, " tsai."

exact and complicated relationships of sonship resulting from ancestor worship, inheritance, concubinage, divorce and remarriage, adoption, etc.

The son, in speaking to the father, calls himself *nan* 男, "a male issue." *Êrh tzŭ* 兒子 is more vocative, and *nan* is principally a literary form of address. During the mourning period the son refers to himself as *ku tzŭ*,[243] *ai tzŭ*,[244] *ku ai tzŭ*,[245] *pu hsiao nan*,[246] or *chi jên*.[247]

The father calls the son *êrh tzŭ* both in the vocative and in writing. In speaking, usually only the name is used. In writing, the relationship term is used together with the name, as " *êrh tzŭ* so and so." This rule applies to relatives of all descending generations.

The complimentary term is *ling lang*.[248] Other combinations are *lang chün*,[249] or *hsien lang*.[250] *Hsien tzŭ*,[251] *ling tzŭ*,[252] and *ling ssŭ* [253] are alternative terms, somewhat more literary. *Kung tzŭ* [254] was originally a term for the sons of the feudal nobility and later for the sons of men of high official positions. But now it has become a general complimentary term almost as prevalent as *ling lang*. Another very common, rather vulgar, term is *shao yêh* 少爺, which also originally referred to the son of a man of rank or of an official, e. g., as used by the servants in referring to the master's son.

The depreciatory term is *hsiao tzŭ*, or *hsiao êrh*. More vulgarly

---

[243] 孤, "orphaned son," used when mourning for the father when the mother is living.

[244] 哀, "grieving son," used when mourning for the mother when the father is chung-piao.

[245] This is used in mourning for either parent when both of them are dead. The differentiation began during the T'ang dynasty. Cf. *Kai yü ts'ung k'ao*, 37. 8a-9b.

[246] 不孝男 " unfilial son."

[247] *Shih Ching* 7B. 3b: 棘人.

[248] 郎 is originally a title of office. During the Han period, high officials could appoint their sons *lang*. Thus *lang* became a complimentary term. Cf. *Ch'êng wei lu*, 6. 3a.

[249] *Yü t'ai hsin yung chi*, 1. 18b.

[250] 古文苑, *Ssŭ pu ts'ung kan* ed., 10. 17a.

[251] *Wei Wu-ti chih* 43a-b.

[252] *Nan Shih* 59. 6a.

[253] *Mo Chi*, 2. 12b.

[254] *Shih Shing* 1C. 6b; *ibid*. 13A. 5a.

hsiao ch'üan 小犬, "a little dog." *Chien hsi*[255] and *jo hsi*[256] are obsolete literary terms.

122. Tzŭ fu 子婦 s w

Hsi fu 媳婦 is a more colloquial term. *Hsi* 媳 was originally written 息, which means "son" or "child." During the Sung period the female classifier was added, forming 媳.[257] Thus it became a distinct term for daughter-in-law. *Hsi fu* may be used for the wives of all the relatives of descending generations.

Son's wife is usually addressed with this name by her parents-in-law. The father-in-law sees her only on formal occasions, and usually maintains a proper distance. When the daughter-in-law gets older and has children, the parents-in-law may even use the grandchildren's term in referring to her—extreme extension of teknonymy.

123. Nü 女 daughter

Nü tzŭ tzŭ[258] and *fu jên tzŭ*[259] are used in the *Li Chi* and *I Li* for daughter, in distinction to *chang fu tzŭ* for male child. *Ying*[260] is said to have been an ancient term for daughter, but this is by no means certain.

Nü êrh is more colloquial. It is used both by parents and daughter, and is a general term as well. When the daughter writes to her parents only *nü* is used in referring to herself.

The complimentary terms are *ling yüan*,[261] *ling ai*,[262] *nü kung tzŭ* 女公子 and, more colloquially, *ch'ien chin*[263] and *hsiao chieh*.[264] *Yü nü*[265] was used during the feudal period, but is no longer used

---

[255] *Shih Chi* 43. 32b: 賤息.
[256] *Nan Shih* 46. 10a: 弱息.
[257] Cf. *Ch'êng wei lu*, 8. 17b-18a.
[258] *I Li* 31. 16b-17a. *Li Chi* 2. 13b.
[259] *I Li* 32. 4a.
[260] *Yü p'ien*: 嬰. It is usually a term for infant.
[261] 令媛 *yüan* is a term for a beautiful girl and *ling yüan* is probably derived from *Shih Ching*, 3A. 5a.
[262] 令愛, your beloved one.
[263] 千金, "a thousand taels of gold," that is precious. *Yin p'ao sui pi* 音飽隨筆, by Tsao Mou-chien 曹枃堅 [乙亥叢編 edition] 8a.
[264] 小姐 was used during the Sung period as a term for young maid servants, or prostitutes. Cf. *Kai yü ts'ung k'ao*, 38. 12. At present it is used as a complimentary term for the daughter of another and for any young woman.
[265] *Li Chi*, 49. 3a: 玉女.

in this sense. *Hsiao niang tzŭ* was commonly used during the T'ang and Sung periods.[266]

The depreciatory terms are *hsiao nü*, more vulgarly, *hsiao ya t'ou* 小丫頭, " little handmaid." *Hsi nü*[267] is an old obsolete term, which could be used as a literary form. *Chia tzŭ*[268] was admissible during the Han period, but was never used in this sense in later times and nowadays is used as a depreciatory term for older sister.

124. Nü hsü 女壻 d h

Mencius uses the term *shêng*. The *Êrh Ya* uses the term *hsü*, which may also mean "husband" in general.[269] *Hsü* is combined with a variety of qualifiers to signify daughter's husband, e. g., *tzŭ hsü*,[270] *lang hsü*, and *hsü shêng*.[271] Other alternative terms are *nü fu*[272] and *pan tzŭ*.[273] *Chiao k'o*,[274] *tung ch'uang*,[275] *t'an ch'uang*,[276] *k'uai hsü*, *chia hsü*,[277] and *mi ch'in*[278] are mostly literary forms, used more or less in a complimentary way.

Ch'ing[279] was originally a dialectical form (Shantung) for daughter's husband, and later was commonly used as a literary term. The forms *tsu pien* 卒便 and *p'ing shih* 平使 are erroneous derivatives of *ch'ing*.[280] *Ch'ing* is also used to mean "husband" in general. *Ch'ing* and *hsü* were originally complimentary terms for a man of ability.

---

[266] Cf. *Kai yü ts'ung k'ao*, 38. 1a.
[267] *Shih Chi*, 8. 4a: 息女.
[268] *Yen shih chia hsün*, 2. 5a: 家⊙. [No. 10, p. 149.]
[269] Originally, it was a complimentary term for an able scholar.
[270] *Shih Chi* 89. 10a.
[271] ⊙ (*Ch'êng wei lu*, 8. 21b). [No. 14, p. 149.]
[272] *Chin Shu* 34. 8a.
[273] 半子, half son. *Liu pin-k'o wên chi*, 外集, 祭虢州楊庶子文, 10. 7.
[274] 嬌客 literally, "delicate" or "graceful guest." It is non-vocative and non-referential.
[275] 東牀 "the one who occupies the bed in the eastern chamber," is based on the anecdote of 王羲之, 東牀坦腹, *Chin Shu* 80. 1b. Cf. *Shih ch'ang t'an*, 1. 3b.
[276] 坦牀.
[277] 快⊙ and 佳⊙ mean practically the same thing. *Pei Shih* 34. 16b-17a.
[278] *Chiu T'ang Shu* 159. 7a: 密親.
[279] *Fang Yen* 3. 1a: 倩.
[280] *Fang Yen*, loc. cit., commentary. *Kuang Ya*, loc. cit.

The complimentary terms are *ling hsü* and *ling t'an*. *Ling t'an* is derived from *t'an ch'uang*, and is rather uncommon.

Depreciatory term, *hsiao hsü*.

125. Chih 姪 b s

The *Êrh Ya* gives no term for brother's son, man speaking. It is conjectured that brother's sons (man speaking) could be called sons, *tzŭ*. The *Li Chi* uses the term *yu tzŭ*, "like son,"[281] but whether or not it is an established term is quite uncertain. During the Han dynasty the term *ts'ung tzŭ*[282] was commonly employed, but more commonly the purely descriptive forms *hsiung tzŭ* and *ti tzŭ* were used. There is evidence that brother's sons were simply called *tzŭ*.[283]

Chih, as used in the *Êrh Ya*, was a woman's term for brother's son. It is similarly used in the *I Li* (32.1b). The use of *chih* as a man's term for brother's son dates from the Chin period (265-420). This usage originated in north China and then became general.[284] The woman's term for brother's son was then prefixed with *nei*, thus forming *nei chih*, in contra-distinction to *chih*.

Chih nan is mostly a self-reference term. *Yüan*[285] is a complimentary term, not commonly used. The common complimentary term is *ling chih*.

126. Chih fu 姪婦 b s w

Chih hsi fu is more colloquial. As remarked above, *hsi fu* applies to the wives of all relatives of descending generations.

127. Chih nü 姪女 b d

Chih as used in the *Êrh Ya* and *I Li* is devoid of sex connotation, a feature characteristic of one of a pair of reciprocal terms.

---

[281] *Li Chi* 8.4a.

[282] *Shih shuo hsin yü*, 1A.21b (commentary): 從子.

[283] *Han shu* 71.4a-b; *Hou Han Shu* 90B.18b: Tsai Yung refers to his father's younger brother and himself as *fu tzŭ*. It also must be understood that whenever one is referring to well-known relationships, or in the vocative, the more inclusive terms *fu tzŭ* are usually used, otherwise the more exact terms.

[284] *Yen shih chia hsün* 2.7a.

[285] 阮 as a complimentary term was based on the uncle-nephew relationship of 阮籍 and 阮咸. Cf. *Shih shuo hsin yü*, 3A.38a.

Ku and *chih* are conceptual reciprocals. When *chih* was transformed into a man's term, it ceased to be reciprocal and the sex indicator was suffixed, e. g., *chih nü* for brother's daughter. The inverted form *nü chih* may also be used. *Yu nü* and *tsʻung nü* are the terms corresponding to *yu tzŭ* and *tsʻung tzŭ*. *Hsiung nü* and *ti nü* are descriptive terms corresponding to *hsiung tzŭ* and *ti tzŭ*.

128. Chih hsü 姪壻 b d h

I hsing[286] is an uncommon ancient term, rarely understood today. *Hsiung hsü*, "older brother's *hsü*," and *ti hsü*, "younger brother's *hsü*," are descriptive alternatives. *Chih nü hsü* is more colloquial.

129. Wai shêng 外甥 si s

The *Êrh Ya* gives the term *chʻu* and, in a later passage, *shêng*. *Chʻu* is probably an older term than *shêng*, since *shêng*, but not *chʻu*, is used in the *I Li*.[287] *Wai shêng* came into use during the Chin dynasty; it is also written 外生.[288] *Chai hsiang*[289] is a term used, probably rarely, circa the first half of the first millennium A. D.

130. Wai shêng fu 外甥婦 si s w

131. Wai shêng nü 外甥女 si d

132. Wai shêng hsü ○○壻 si d h

133. Tʻang chih 堂姪 f b s s

134. Tʻang chih fu ○○婦 f b s s w

135. Tʻang chih nü ○○女 f b s d

[286] *Ta tai li chi*, 6. 7a: 異姓.   [287] *I Li* 33. 9a.
[288] *Shih shuo hsin yü*, 3A. 3a (commentary).
[289] 宅相, "house site," is of interesting origin. *Chin shu* 41. 1a: Wei Shu was an orphan reared in his maternal grandmother's home, the Ning family. When the Ning's built a house, a geomancer prophecied that this house site, *Chai hsiang*, would have a daughter's son who would be great. Wei Shu's maternal grandmother considered this prophecy had been fulfilled, when Wei Shu, although young, was brilliant and precocious. Wei Shu then said, "I will fulfill the prophecy of this good house site, chai hsiang." *Pei Chʻi Shu* 29. 2b; *Shih chʻang tʻan*, 1. 3a.

136. T'ang chih hsü 〇〇壻 f b s d h
137. T'ang wai shêng 堂外甥 f b d s
138. T'ang wai shêng fu 〇〇甥婦 f b d s w
139. T'ang wai shêng nü 〇〇甥女 f b d d
140. T'ang wai shêng hsü 〇〇甥壻 f b d d h
141. Ku piao chih 姑表姪 f si s s
142. Ku piao chih fu 〇〇〇婦 w of 141
143. Ku piao chih nü 〇〇〇女 f si s d
144. Ku piao chih hsü 〇〇〇壻 h of 143
145. Ku piao wai shêng 〇〇外甥 f si d s
146. Ku piao wai shêng fu 〇〇外甥婦 w of 145
147. Ku piao wai shêng nü 〇〇〇〇女 f si d d
148. Ku piao wai shêng hsü 〇〇〇〇壻 h of 147
149. Tsai ts'ung chih 再從姪 s of 89 or 91
150. Tsai ts'ung chih fu 〇〇姪婦 w of 149
151. Tsai ts'ung chih nü 〇〇〇女 d of 89 or 91
152. Tsai ts'ung chih hsü 〇〇〇壻 h of 151
153. Tsu chih 族姪 s of 97 or 99
154. Tsu chih fu 〇〇婦 w of 153
155. Tsu chih nü 〇〇女 d of 97 or 99
156. Tsu chih hsü 〇〇壻 h of 155

VII. Generation of the son's son

157. Sun 孫 s s

Tzŭ hsing [290] is an old obsolete term. During the Chin period

[290] *Shih Ching* 1C. 7a; *I Li* 44. 2b; *Shih Chi* 49. 2a.

wan shêng 晚生, " late born," was used for son, likewise, *hsiao wan shêng*, " little late born," for son's son.[291] *Wên sun* is a literary form derived from the *Book of History*;[292] it originally referred to King Wên's son's son. *Sun êrh* and *sun tzǔ* are more colloquial, *êrh* and *tzǔ* being diminutives.

Chia sun[293] was used as a depreciatory term during the Han period, but has never been used since and is now considered incorrect. The correct depreciatory term is *hsiao sun*.

Sun may be combined with various modifiers to express the exact relationships, e. g., *chang sun* for the oldest son's son, *shih sun* or *ch'êng chung sun*[294] for the eldest son's eldest son, who must carry the three years mourning obligations in his father's place in the event that the father has died before the grandfather.

158. Sun fu 孫婦 s s w

159. Sun nü 孫女 s d

Sun, as in the *I Li*, may be used to mean grandchild or any descendant from the second descending generation and down. In modern usage *sun nü* is employed in contra-distinction to *sun*. The inverted form, *nü sun*, is also permissible.

160. Sun hsü 孫壻 s d h

161. Wai sun 外孫 d s

162. Wai sun fu ○○婦 d s w

163. Wai sun nü ○○女 d d

164. Wai sun hsü ○○壻 d d h

165. Chih sun 姪孫 b s s

Ts'ung sun is a term found in the *Kuo Yü*.[295] *Yu sun*[296] was occasionally used during the T'ang period, and earlier, but is seldom used today, except as a literary form.

[291] *Chin shu* 69. 7b; *P'ieh chi*, 4. 2a.
[292] *Shu Ching* 17. 35a: 文孫.
[293] *Yen shih chia hsün* 2. 5a.
[294] *I Li* 30. 12a: 其適孫承重者.
[295] *Kuo yü* 3. 7a.
[296] *Yüan shih Chang-ch'ing chi* 54. 4b.

HISTORICAL REVIEW OF TERMS 105

166. Chih sun fu ○○婦 b s s w
167. Chih sun nü ○○女 b s d
168. Chih sun hsü ○○壻 b s d h
169. Wai chih sun 外姪孫 b d s
170. Wai chih sun fu ○○○婦 b d s w
171. Wai chih sun nü ○○○女 b d d
172. Wai chih sun hsü ○○○壻 b d d h

In local variations, *chih wai sun* 姪外孫 and *t'ang wai sun* 堂外孫 may be used for 169–172.

173. Wai shêng sun 外甥孫 si s s

The term in the *Êrh Ya* is *li sun* 離孫, literally "departing grandson." Whether or not there is any significance in this term one cannot say. Other ancient alternative terms are *ts'ung sun shêng*[297] and *mi sun*.[298]

174. Wai shêng sun fu 外甥孫婦 si s s w
175. Wai shêng sun nü ○○孫女 si s d
176. Wai shêng sun hsü ○○孫壻 si s d h
177. T'ang chih sun 堂姪孫 f b s s s
178. T'ang chih sun fu ○○○婦 w of 177
179. T'ang chih sun nü ○○○女 f b s s d
180. T'ang chih sun hsü ○○○壻 h of 179
181. Ku piao chih sun 姑表姪孫 f si s s s
182. Ku piao chih sun fu ○○○○婦 w of 181
183. Ku piao chih sun nü ○○○○女 f si s s d
184. Ku piao chih sun hsü ○○○○壻 h of 183
185. Tsai ts'ung chih sun 再從姪孫 s of 149

---

[297] *Tso Chuan* 60.20b.   [298] *Ibid* 60.17b: 彌.

186. Tsai ts'ung chih sun fu ○○○○婦 w of 185

187. Tsai ts'ung chih sun nü ○○○○女 d of 149

188. Tsai ts'ung chih sun hsü ○○○○壻 h of 187

189. Tsu sun 族孫 s of 153

190. Tsu sun fu ○○婦 w of 189

191. Tsu sun nü ○○女 d of 153

192. Tsu sun hsü ○○壻 h of 191

Tsu chih sun 族姪孫 may be used in substitution for *tsu sun* in terms 189-192, but the *chih* is not necessary.

VIII. Generation of the son's son's son

193. Tsêng sun 曾孫 s s s

According to old usages all descendants from the son's son's son and descending can be called *tsêng sun*, or *hsi sun*.[298a] During the Han period *êrh sun* was probably used synonymously with *tsêng sun*.[299]

Ch'ung sun 重孫 is the modern colloquial term.

194. Tsêng sun fu 曾孫婦 s s s w

195. Tsêng sun nü 曾孫女 s s d

196. Tsêng sun hsü ○○壻 s s d h

197. Wai sun tsêng sun 外孫曾孫 d s s, or s d s

198. Wai sun tsêng sun nü ○○○○女 d s d, or s d d

199. Tsêng chih sun 曾姪孫 b s s s

200. Tsêng chih sun nü ○○○女 b s s d

[298a] *Chiu T'ang shu* 160. 19b.

[299] *Han Shu* 2. 2b. The interpretations of the term *êrh sun* 耳孫 are quite divergent. Perhaps the interpretation of 李裴 is the more prevalent usage in the Han period but it by no means precludes its use in the other connotations. Cf. *Hsüeh Lin* 3. 10-11.

201. Wai shêng tsêng sun 外甥曾孫 si s s s

202. Wai shêng tsêng sun nü ○○○○女 si s s d

IX. Generation of the son's son's son's son

203. Hsüan sun 玄孫 [300] s s s s

204. Hsüan sun fu ○○婦 s s s s w

205. Hsüan sun nü ○○女 s s s d

206. Hsüan sun hsü ○○壻 s s s d h

The following terms are found in the *Êrh Ya*; although of no practical use, they are given here because of their theoretical interest:

207. Lai sun 來孫 s s s s s

208. K'un sun 昆○ s s s s s s

209. Jêng sun 仍○ s s s s s s s

210. Yün sun 雲○ s s s s s s s s

Consanguineal Relatives—Table II

Relatives Through Mother

I. Generation of the mother's father's father

1. Wai tsêng tsu fu 外曾祖父 m f f

   In the *Êrh Ya* the term is *wai tsêng wang fu* ○○王父.

2. Wai tsêng tsu mu ○○祖母 m f m

   Wai tsêng wang mu ○○王母, as used in the *Êrh Ya*. Vocatives of the above two terms vary locally; they are largely based on the vocatives of 3 and 4, with generation modifiers.

II. Generation of the mother's father

3. Wai tsu fu 外祖父 m f

   Wai tsu may be used alone. The term in the *Êrh Ya* is *wai*

[300] *Jih Chih lu*, 5. 32b.

wang fu 外王父. *Wai ta fu*[1] and *wai wêng*[2] are modern alternatives. The modern vocatives *chia kung*,[3] also pronounced *ka kung*, and *wai kung* were used as early as the fifth century A. D.

4. Wai tsu mu 外祖母 m m

Wai wang mu is used in the *Êrh Ya*. *Wai p'o*[4] is the most common modern vocative; likewise common is *chia p'o*, also pronounced *ka p'o*. *Chia mu*[5] was used during the fifth and sixth centuries A. D. Since *chia* at that time meant "mother," *chia mu* meant mother's mother. *Chia mu* is now used as a depreciatory term for mother. *Liao liao*[6] is a dialectical form used in certain parts of North China.

5. Wai po tsu fu 外伯祖父 m f o b

6. Wai po tsu mu ○○○母 m f o b w

7. Wai shu tsu fu 外叔祖父 m f y b

8. Wai shu tsu mu ○○○母 m f y b w

Ku wai tsu mu may be used for the mother's father's sister, *chiu wai tsu fu* for the mother's mother's brother, and *i wai tsu mu* for the mother's mother's sister. These relationships are not maintained socially, but the terms show how they can be handled. Practically, there are many ways of solving this terminological problem, e. g., if the necessity for addressing these relatives should arise, one may adopt the terms of the mother's brother's son, who is the nearest relative of the same generation of ego on the mother's side.

[1] *Chang Yu-shih wên chi* 張右史文集, collected works of CHANG Lei 張耒 (1052-1112 A. D.), *Ssŭ pu ts'ung k'an* edition, 17. 9b.
[2] *Yüan shih chang-ch'ing chi* 9. 5b.
[3] *Yen shih chia hsün* 2. 8a.
[4] *Jung chai sui pi, ssŭ pi* 2. 11a.
[5] See note 3.
[6] *K'ang-hsi tzŭ tien* 嬢. *Liao* is also read *lao*, and is synonymous with *ao*. YEN Chih-t'ui [*Yen shih chia hsün*, 2. 7b] says that during his time the uncultured people called mother's parents by the same terms as father's parents when the latter were all dead.

III. Generation of the mother

9. Chiu fu 舅父 m b

Or simply *chiu*, as used in the *Êrh Ya*. Since in modern usage, *chiu* also means wife's brother, the generation and sex indicator *fu* is necessary. *Po chiu* 伯舅 may be used for the mother's older brother, and *shu chiu* 权舅 for the younger brother. These terms are now mainly literary. The mother's brothers and their family may be vaguely referred to as *wai shih* or *wai chia*.[7]

Vocatives are *chiu chiu, a chiu,* or *chiu tieh. Chia chiu* [8] was used as a depreciatory term during the fourth and fifth centuries A. D., but is not used today and is considered incorrect. *Ling chiu* and *tsun chiu* are complimentary terms.

10. Chiu mu 舅母 m b w

Chin [9] is an old vocative used during the Sung period, and is now rather uncommon. The modern vocative is *chiu ma*.

11. I mu 姨母 m si

In the *Êrh Ya* and the *I Li* the term is *ts'ung mu*.[10] *I* originally meant "wife's sister." The first use of *i* for mother's sister is found in the *Tso Chuan*, the 23rd year (B. C. 550) of Duke Hsiang.[11] This extension is attributed to the psychological similarity of these two relatives and to reverse teknonymy. Since the Han period *i* has entirely displaced the older term *ts'ung mu*. *I* is also used for concubines—a usage attributed to the sororate. The inverted form *mu i* may also be used.

Vocatives are *a i* or *i ma*.

12. I fu 姨父 m si h

I fu,[12] *i chang jên*,[13] or *i chang*, were used during the first millennium A. D., but are uncommon today.

---

[7] Literally "outer family." *Chin Shu* 41.1a.
[8] *Shih shuo hsin yü*, 3B.32a.
[9] *Shu I*, 1.9b: 姶. *Ming t'ao tsa chih*, 13b.
[10] *I Li* 33.2a.
[11] *Tso Chuan* 35.18a.   [12] *Yen shih chia hsün* 3.23a.
[13] *Pei Shih* 47.7b-8a. *I chang jên* is now used to mean wife's mother's sister's husband.

13. T'ang chiu fu 堂舅父 m f b s

Ts'ung chiu is used in the *Êrh Ya* and can still be used today, but more as a literary form.

14. T'ang chiu mu 堂舅母 w of 13

15. T'ang i mu 堂姨母 m f b d

16. T'ang i fu 堂姨父 h of 15

IV. Generation of the speaker

17. Chiu piao hsiung 舅表兄 m b s > e

Shêng is the term in the *Êrh Ya*—a reflection of cross-cousin marriage. *Nei hsiung*[14] was a substitute used during the Han period; later it became confused with *wai hsiung*,[15] a term for father's sister's son. Today these terms are not used with the same meanings. *Nei hsiung* is now used for the wife's older brother, and *wai hsiung* for half brothers, by the same mother, older than ego. *Chiu tzŭ*[16] and *chiu ti*[17] are purely descriptive terms which were used *circa* 500 A.D.; at present they both mean " wife's brothers."

Piao was first introduced during the latter part of the Han period, after cross-cousin marriage had long ceased to be preferential. *Piao*, or *chung piao*,[18] was first used for mother's brother's and father's sister's children, and later was extended to include mother's sister's children.

In the vocative *chiu* is always dropped, leaving simply *piao hsiung* or *piao ko*, and, in certain localities, *lao piao*.

18. Chiu piao sao 舅表嫂 w of 17

19. Chiu piao ti ○○弟 m b s < e

20. Chiu piao ti fu ○○弟婦 w of 19

21. Chiu piao tzŭ ○○姊 m b d > e

22. Chiu piao tzŭ fu ○○姊夫 h of 21

---

[14] *I Li* 33. 10a.
[15] *Sung shu* 93. 4b-5a.
[16] *Chin Shu* 34. 8b.
[17] *Ch'ang-li Chi* 32. 7b.
[18] *San kuo chih* 11. 20. *Chung piao* is equivalent to *nei wai*.

23. Chiu piao mei ○○妹 m b d ⟨ e
24. Chiu piao mei fu ○○妹夫 h of 23
25. I piao hsiung 姨表兄 m si s ⟩ e

Ts'ung mu k'un ti is used in the *Êrh Ya* and *I Li* (33.9a). *I hsiung ti* was used during the last few centuries of the first millennium B.C. and approximately the first half of the first millennium A.D.[19] It can still today be used as an alternative term.[20] *Wai hsiung ti* was sometimes used during the T'ang period,[21] having resulted from a confusion with the term for mother's brother's sons and father's sister's sons, which finally led to the extension of the term *piao* and the partial merging of the three relationships.

26. I piao sao 姨表嫂 w of 25
27. I piao ti ○○弟 m si s ⟨ e
28. I piao ti fu ○○弟婦 w of 27
29. I piao tzŭ ○○姊 m si d ⟩ e
30. I piao tzŭ fu ○○姊夫 h of 29
31. I piao mei ○○妹 m si d ⟨ e
32. I piao mei fu ○○妹夫 h of 31
33. T'ang chiu piao hsiung 堂舅表兄 m f b s s ⟩ e
34. T'ang chiu piao sao ○○○嫂 w of 33
35. T'ang chiu piao ti ○○○弟 m f b s s ⟨ e
36. T'ang chiu piao ti fu ○○○弟婦 w of 35
37. T'ang chiu piao tzŭ 堂舅表姊 m f b s d ⟩ e
38. T'ang chiu piao tzŭ fu ○○○○夫 h of 37

---

[19] See discussion, pp. 177-178. *Nan shih* 57.17a.
[20] Cf. LIANG Chang-chü, *Ch'êng wei lu*, 3.20b. WANG Shih-han 汪師韓, 1707-? A.D., considers *i hsiung ti* a northern peculiarity: *T'an shu lu* 談書錄, (昭代叢書 ed.) 45a.
[21] 海錄碎事 (cited by *Ch'êng wei lu*, 3.20a).

39. T'ang chiu piao mei 堂舅表妹 m f b s d < e

40. T'ang chiu piao mei fu ○○○○夫 h of 39

Terms 33-40 may also be applied to the children of father's mother's brother's sons, i. e., the children of 59-62 in table I, hence these terms are not given there. This extension is inferred only from popular usage, there being insufficient documentary evidence for collation. At any rate, when one considers non-sib relatives on the third collateral line in as far as the third generation descending, the terminology becomes vague, and, indeed, an accurate system is not necessary here, since in almost all cases these relationships are not maintained socially.

41. T'ang i piao hsiung 堂姨表兄 m f b d s > e

42. T'ang i piao sao ○○表嫂 w of 41

43. T'ang i piao ti ○○表弟 m f b d s < e

44. T'ang i piao ti fu ○○表弟婦 w of 43

45. T'ang i piao tzǔ 堂姨表姊 m f b d d > e

46. T'ang i piao tzǔ fu ○○表姊夫 h of 45

47. T'ang i piao mei ○○表妹 m f b d d < e

48. T'ang i piao mei fu ○○表妹夫 h of 47

V. Generation of the son

49. Chiu piao chih 舅表姪 m b s s

50. Chiu piao chih fu ○○○婦 m b s s w

51. Chiu piao chih nü ○○○女 m b s d

52. Chiu piao chih hsü ○○○○壻 m b s d h

53. Chiu piao wai-shêng 舅表外甥 m b d s

54. Chiu piao wai-shêng fu ○○○○婦 m b d s w

55. Chiu piao wai-shêng-nü ○○○○女 m b d d

56. Chiu piao wai-shêng hsü 〇〇〇〇壻 m b d d h
57. I piao chih 姨表姪 m si s s
58. I piao chih fu 〇〇〇婦 m si s s w
59. I piao chih nü 〇〇〇女 m si s d
60. I piao chih hsü 〇〇〇壻 m si s d h
61. I piao wai shêng 〇〇外甥 m si d s
62. I piao wai-shêng fu 〇〇〇〇婦 m si d s w
63. I piao wai-shêng nü 舅表外甥女 m si d d
64. I piao wai-shêng hsü 〇〇〇〇壻 m si d d h
65. T'ang chiu piao chih 堂舅表姪 s of 33 or 35
66. T'ang chiu piao chih fu 〇〇〇〇婦 w of 65
67. T'ang chiu piao chih nü 〇〇〇〇女 d of 33 or 35
68. T'ang chiu piao chih hsü 〇〇〇〇壻 h of 67
69. T'ang i piao chih 堂姨表姪 s of 41 or 43
70. T'ang i piao chih fu 〇〇〇〇婦 w of 69
71. T'ang i piao chih nü 〇〇〇〇女 d of 41 or 43
72. T'ang i piao chih hsü 〇〇〇〇壻 h of 71

VI. Generation of the son's son

73. Chiu piao chih sun 舅表姪孫 m b s s s
74. Chiu piao chih sun fu 〇〇〇〇婦 m b s s s w
75. Chiu piao chih sun nü 〇〇〇〇女 m b s s d
76. Chiu piao chih sun hsü 〇〇〇〇壻 m b s s d h
77. I piao chih sun 姨表姪孫 m si s s s
78. I piao chih sun fu 〇〇〇〇婦 m si s s s w

79. I piao chih sun nü ◎◎◎◎女 m si s s d

80. I piao chih sun hsü ◎◎◎◎婿 m si s s d h

Since most of these terms are extensions from table I, their historical development, vocative and complimentary usages can be inferred from there.

Affinal Relatives—Table III

Relatives Through Wife

I. Generation of the wife's father

1. Yo fu 岳父 w f

The term in the *Êrh Ya* is *wai chiu*, and in the *Li Chi* (52. 27b), *chiu* is used alone for this relationship. As *chiu* also meant mother's brother during this period, the terminology reflects cross-cousin marriage. During the Later Han period *fu kung*[1] and *fu wêng*[2] were prevailingly used, as purely descriptive terms. Whether or not *chang jên* 丈人 was used for wife's father during the Han period is by no means clear;[3] it became the prevailing term during the T'ang dynasty.[4] *Yo fu* and *chang jên* are the universal modern terms, and the use of the one or the other depends upon local custom. *Yo fu* is more formal and literary, *chang jên* is more colloquial. Sometimes the combined and abbreviated form *yo chang* is used. Another very common but non-vocative and non-referential term is *t'ai shan*, name of the eastern sacred mountain of the old Chinese Empire. There are many interpretations of the origin of the terms *yo fu*, *chang jên* and *t'ai shan*, of interest to those who are concerned with the origin of individual terms.

One interpretation of the origin of the term *yo* is that found in the *Chiao ssŭ chih* of the *Han Shu* (25A. 13a), viz., large mountains are called *yo shan*, and small mountains, *yo hsü*. Since mountains can be called both *yo* and *hsü*, and since *hsü* also means daughter's

---

[1] *Hou Han Shu* 71. 11a.   [2] *San Kuo Chih* 1. 22b-23a.

[3] *Han Shu* 94A. 25b-26a. In the *Nêng kai chai man lu*, 2. 28, this erroneously considered to be the origin of *chang jên* for wife's father. The term *chang jên* used here merely means any older man; cf. Yen Shih-ku's commentary on this passage.

[4] *Chiu T'ang Shu* 147. 1b.

husband, the meaning of *yo* was transferred and *yo* became a term for wife's father.[5] Another interpretation goes thus: Yo Kuang of the Chin dynasty was the father of the wife of Wei Chieh; since these two men were the best-known personages of their time, and since their relationship as father-in-law and son-in-law was much admired by the people, it is possible that *yo chang* 岳丈 is a corruption of *Yo chang* 樂丈 [6]

The story of the origin of the term *t'ai shan* is as follows: In the year 725 A. D. the Emperor Hsüan-tsung offered sacrifices to T'ai Shan, "Mount T'ai." According to precedence, all those officials who participated in it, with the exception of the San Kung 三公, were promoted one rank. Chang Yüeh, the premier, was the marshal of ceremonies. This son-in-law, Chêng I, was promoted from the ninth rank to the fifth rank and was accorded the privilege of wearing purple robes. In the banquet of celebration the Emperor was surprised by his quick advancement. The professional court jester, Huang Fa-cho, remarked: "This is the influence of T'ai Shan!" This is popularly considered the explanation of the origin of the term.[7] But *t'ai shan* must already have had the meaning of father-in-law, since this joke is a pun, *t'ai shan* being interpreted both as wife's father and as Mount T'ai; i. e., Chêng I's unprecedented promotion was due to his participation in the sacrifices to T'ai Shan, or, in a satirical sense, to the influence of his father-in-law, Chang Yüeh.

Still another version of the origin of the terms *t'ai shan* and *yo* relates that Mount T'ai, also called Eastern Yo, has a peak named Chang Jên. Since *chang jên* means wife's father, and Chang Jên is one of the peaks of T'ai Shan, *t'ai shan* has become a term for wife's father—a kind of punning and semantic transference. Furthermore, T'ai Shan is also called Yo, whence the term *yo* is derived.[8]

These are interesting speculations, any one of which is just as reasonable as any other. One point seems to be certain, viz., that

---

[5] *Jih sun chai pi chi* 日損齋筆記 by 黃溍 [1277-1357 A. D.] [墨海金壺 edition] 10b.

[6] *Chin Shu* 36. 13b; *Kai yü ts'ung k'ao* 37. 20a.

[7] Cf. *Shih ch'ang t'an* 1. 2b.   [8] *Kai yü ts'ung k'ao* 37. 20a.

no sociological factors or marital implications are involved. First, from the linguistic point of view, both *yo* and *tʻai shan* have never been used in any sense other than " venerable high mountain " and " Mount Tʻai." Second, as relationship terms, both of them are late introductions, not earlier than the Tʻang period. If there were any sociological implications, they should be easily detectable.

The application of *chang jên* to wife's father, as remarked above, first became prevalent during the Tʻang period. Before and during the Han periods it could be applied to any old man to whom one might wish to pay respect. From the fourth to the sixth centuries A. D. *chang jên* was used for mother's brother, mother's sister's husband and father's sister's husband, e. g., *chung wai chang jên*. Hence, its use for wife's father may be an alternative extension from the term *chiu*, which was used during this period for mother's brother and sometimes for wife's father. If this idea is correct, the use of *chang jên* may be an indirect survival from cross-cousin marriage.

Wai fu,[9] *ping sou*,[10] and *ping wêng*,[11] were alternative terms used during the Sung period. *Fu tʻo*[12] is an old dialectal term used in southwest China during the Han period.

Chia yo is used as a depreciatory term, but theoretically it may be incorrect.

2. Yo mu 岳母 w m

Wai ku or *ku* alone are used in the *Êrh Ya* and *Li Chi*—a reflection of cross-cousin marriage. *Chang mu* and *tʻai shui*[13] are terms corresponding to *chang jên* and *tʻai shan*. Before the Tʻang

---

[9] Cf. *Chʻien chü lu* 潛居錄 [*Shuo Fu* 說郛, 32] 1b.
[10] *Tung pʻo chʻüan chi* 東坡全集, Ssŭ pu pei yao ed., 13. 7: 氷叟.
[11] *Yu huan chi wên* 游宦紀聞, by Chang Shih-nan 張世南 (ca. 1200 A.D.), 知不足齋叢書本 6. 2b. On *ping sou* and *ping wêng* see p. 255, note 6.
[12] *Fang Yen*, 6. 7a: ⊙女多.
[13] 合璧事類 (cited by the *Chʻêng wei lu*, 7. 13a): 泰水. The term *tʻai shui* is really interesting. The opposite of *shan*, mountain, is *shui*, water. Water is here used in the sense of " rivers " or " lakes." Since wife's father is called *tʻai shan*, so *tʻai shui* is used for wife's mother. The *Ho pi shih lei* being a cyclopaedia compiled during the Sung period, the term must have been quite common during that time. At present it is not a very good term and employed mostly on non-vocative and non-referential occasions.

period, *chang mu* could be applied to father's and mother's married sisters, mother's brother's wife, or the wife of any person whom one addressed as *chang jên*. *Mu tʻo*[14] was a dialectal form corresponding to *fu tʻo*.

Yo fu and *yo mu* may be used vocatively, but generally the husband adopts the wife's terms, addressing her parents with parent terms. Post-issue, teknonymy is the most common practice.

In referring to wife's father's parents, circumlocution by enumeration of relations is common. In certain localities *lao chang jên* and *lao chang mu* are used in the referential. Inferentially and logically, *yo tsu fu* and *yo tsu mu* would be correct, but they are not used. In the vocative, one usually adopts the wife's terms.

3. Po yo fu 伯岳父 w f o b
4. Po yo mu 伯岳母 w f o b w
5. Shu yo fu 叔岳父 w f y b
6. Shu yo mu 叔岳母 w f y b w

Alternatively and more commonly, *po chang jên* is used for 3, *po chang mu* for 4, *shu chang jên* for 5, and *shu chang mu* for 6. *Lieh yo*[15] is an uncommon complimentary term for 3 and 5.

Wife's father's sister and her husband are called *ku chang mu* and *ku chang jên*, wife's mother's sister and her husband are called *i chang mu* and *i chang jên*, and wife's mother's brother and his wife, *chiu chang jên* and *chiu chang mu*, respectively.

II. Generation of the wife

7. Chiu hsiung 舅兄 w o b

Shêng, which is used in the *Êrh Ya*, reflects cross-cousin marriage. The *Êrh Ya* also gives the term *hun hsiung ti*, "brothers by marriage" a purely descriptive term. The *Li Chi*[16] gives the term *ssŭ chʻin hsiung ti*, also more or less descriptive, since *ssŭ chʻin* literally means "private relations." *Fu hsiung ti*[17] and *nei*

---

[14] Cf. *Fang yen* 6. 7a.
[15] *Ho pi shih lei* (cited by *Chʻêng wei Lu* 7. 13a), 列嶽.
[16] *Li Chi* 27. 11b. [17] See p. 195, note 84.

hsiung ti [18] were in use from the Chin to the T'ang dynasties, and can still be used as alternative terms. *Fu* and *nei* both mean "wife." *Chiu* was first applied during the tenth century A. D., through teknonymy.[19]

8. Chiu sao 舅嫂 w o b w

Ch'i sao [20] may be used, but is a purely descriptive term.

9. Chiu ti 舅弟 w y b

10. Chiu ti fu 舅弟婦 w y b w

11. I tzŭ 姨姊 w o si

12. I tzŭ fu 姨姊夫 w o si h

The term in the *Êrh Ya* for wife's sisters' husbands is *ya* [21] or *yin ya* as used in the *Shih Ching*.[22] *Yu hsü* [23] was used during the Han period and *t'ung mên* a little later.[24] *Liao hsü* originated as a local term in eastern China. *Lien mei* and *lien chin* [25] were first used during the Sung period. *Lien chin* is the most commonly used term at present; it probably originated as a local form in North China. *I fu*,[26] as a term, is as old as any of those above, but more descriptive. These terms are used reciprocally, i. e., ego refers to his wife's sisters' husbands by any of these terms, according to local usage, and they refer to him by precisely the same term. These terms are only used in the referential. Vocatively, brother terms are usually adopted, or teknonymy is practiced.

13. I mei 姨妹 w y si

Ch'i mei [27] and *nei mei* [28] are alternative and principally de-

---

[18] *Liang Shu* 12.4a; *Chin shih ts'ui pien* 101.26a. The use of *nei hsiung ti* for wife's brothers was confused with that for mother's brother's sons. It may be due to the influence of earlier cross-cousin marriage terminology from which the new nomenclature still could not extricate itself.

[19] See discussion pp. 194-197.

[20] *Nan shih* 45.13b.

[21] 亞.

[22] *Shih Ching* 12A.3b: 姻亞.

[23] *Han Shu* 64A.10b: 友婿.

[24] *Êrh Ya*: 同門, 僚⊙.

[25] *Luan chên tzŭ lu*, 嬾眞子錄, by MA Yung-ch'ing 馬永卿, ca. 1110 A.D. [1920, Commercial Press ed.] 2.5b: 連袂, 連襟.

[26] *Ho pi shih lei* [cited by *Ch'êng wei Lu* 7.17a-b).

[27] *San kuo chih* 22.1b.

[28] *Ibid.* 9.6a.

scriptive terms. *I*, as used in the *Êrh Ya*, is interpreted as meaning the wife's sisters who have married different men, and most probably it was originally a man's term.²⁹ *Ti* 娣 is used to mean sisters who have married the same man in connection with the *yin* marriage custom, and is more likely to be a woman's term.³⁰ *Hsiao i* is a modern colloquial expression.

14. I mei fu 姨妹夫 w y si h
15. T'ang chiu hsiung 堂舅兄 s of 3 or 5 > w
16. T'ang chiu sao ◎◎嫂 w of 15
17. T'ang chiu ti ◎◎弟 s of 3 or 5 < w
18. T'ang chiu ti fu ◎◎弟婦 w of 17
19. T'ang i tzŭ 堂姨姊 d of 3 or 5 > w
20. T'ang i tzŭ fu ◎◎姊夫 h of 19
21. T'ang i mei ◎◎妹 d of 3 or 5 < w
22. T'ang i mei fu ◎◎妹夫 h of 21

Wife's father's sister's children, wife's mother's sister's and brother's children are called *nei piao hsiung ti* for males, and *nei piao tzŭ mei* for females. It could be further differentiated by adding *ku*, *i* and *chiu*, e. g., *nei ku piao hsiung* for wife's father's sister's son older than wife.

III. Generation of the son

23. Nei chih 內姪 w b s

Chih was originally a woman's term for brother's child, being reciprocal with *ku*. Since the Chin period it has been used more as a man's term for brother's son, hence *nei* is prefixed, in contradistinction with *chih* alone. See Table I, 125. In contemporary usage, female ego would use *chih* for brother's son before marriage,

---

²⁹ *Shih Ching* 3B.9a; *Tso Chuan* 8.24a.
³⁰ *Shih Ching* 18D.5a. Cf. the *Shih ming*. It seems the term *ti* cannot be separated from the *yin* marriage custom. Accordingly, when the *yin* marriage ceased to be practiced, *ti* also ceased to function.

but after marriage she would use *chih* for husband's brother's son and *nei chih* for her own brother's son.

24. Nei chih fu ◎◎婦 w b s w
25. Nei chih nü ◎◎女 w b d
26. Nei chih hsü ◎◎壻 w b d h
27. I wai shêng 姨外甥 w si s

Ch'i shêng[31] was used *circa* sixth century A. D. It is more or less descriptive, i. e., wife's *shêng*.

28. I wai shêng fu ◎◎甥婦 w si s w
29. I wai shêng nü ◎◎甥女 w si d
30. I wai shêng hsü ○○甥壻 w si d h

In certain local usages *i chih* may be substituted for *i wai shêng* in terms 27-30. Although illogical, it is permitted locally.

IV. Generation of the son's son

31. Nei chih sun 內姪孫 w b s s

The *Êrh Ya* uses the term *kuei sun*, which literally means "returning grandson." *Kuei sun* was probably a woman's term, since the *Êrh Ya* says that *chih*'s sons are called *kuei sun*, and *chih* is primarily a woman's term in the *Êrh Ya*.

32. Nei chih sun fu □□□婦 w b s s w
33. Nei chih sun nü □□□女 w b s d
34. Nei chih sun hsü □□□壻 w b s d h
35. I wai shêng sun: w si s s [32]
36. I wai shêng sun fu: w si s s w
37. I wai shêng sun nü: w si s d
38. I wai shêng sun hsü: w si s d h

---

[31] *Liang Shu* 28. 2a.
[32] For characters, see Nos. 24-30 above.

In some local usages *i chih sun* may be substituted for *i wai shêng sun*. Terms 23 to 38 are used by husband and female ego alike.

Affinal Relatives—Table IV

Relatives Through Husband

I. Generation of the husband's father

1. Kung 公 h f

In the *Êrh Ya* the general term is *chiu*; when he is living, *chün chiu* [1] is used—a reflection of cross-cousin marriage. In modern ritual works, the compilers still use *chiu* for husband's father and refuse to employ the modern term *kung*. If they are afraid lest the term be misunderstood, they employ the descriptive nomenclature, e. g., *fu* of *fu* 夫之父 " father of husband " or *mu* of *fu* 夫之母 " mother of husband."

Chang [2] and *chung* [3] were used during and somewhat before the Han period. *Kuan* [4] was a local term in the lower Yangtze valley *circa* the end of the T'ang dynasty. All these terms seem to have been more or less local, and their degree of prevalence is uncertain. The modern term *kung* dates from about the fourth and fifth centuries A. D.; [5] it is also used in the doubled form *kung kung*.

Hsien chiu,[6] *huang chiu*,[7] and *hsien tzŭ* [8] are old posthumous terms no longer used today.

2. P'o 婆 h m

Ku, and *chün ku* only when she is living, are the terms used in the *Êrh Ya*—a reflection of cross-cousin marriage. *Wei* [9] was used during the Han period, and *wei ku* [10] is equivalent to *chün*

---

[1] *Êrh Ya*: 君舅.
[2] *Shih Ming*: 章.
[3] *Lü Shih ch'un ch'iu* 14.17a: 公.
[4] *Nan T'ang Shu* [by Ma Ling] 25.2a: 官.
[5] *Yü t'ai hsin yung chi* 1.16a-21a.
[6] See note 1.
[7] *I Li* 6.1a-2b.
[8] *Kuo Yü* 5.9b: 先子.
[9] *Shuo Wên*: 威.
[10] Wang Nien-Sun [*Kuang ya su chêng* 6B.5]: 威姑.

ku of the *Êrh Ya*. *Chia*, or *a chia*,[11] are terms used *circa* the fourth and fifth centuries A. D. and surviving quite late as dialectal forms. *Mu*[12] was also used *circa* 500 A. D. *P'o* in ancient usage may mean any old woman; its use for husband's mother dates from the T'ang period. The use of *kung* and *p'o* for husband's parents might also be due to teknonymy, since from quite early times *kung* and *p'o* have commonly been used as grandparents' terms.

Huang ku and *hsien ku* are ancient posthumous terms.

II. Generation of the husband

3. Pên shên 本身 ego, a female

Ego, a female, might, in speaking to the husband's relatives, refer to herself as *hsin fu*, during the fourth and fifth centuries A. D.[13] This custom seems to have been in vogue as late as the twelfth century A. D.[14] At present, the proper relationship term should be used.

4. Fu 夫 husband

Chang fu 丈夫 and *fu hsü* are alternative terms. *Hsü* may be used alone for husband. *Lao kung*[15] and *nan jên*[16] are colloquial rather vulgar, terms.

Whether or not *shih*,[17] *po*,[18] *tzŭ*,[19] *chün tzŭ*,[20] *fu tzŭ*,[21] and *chia*[22] are actually ancient relationship terms for husband can-

---

[11] *Pei Ch'i Shu* 30. 4b. *Nan shih* 33. 9a. The *chia* may be a different rendering of *ku*, as they may be pronounced about the same. Cf. *Yen shih chia hsün* 1. 14a.

[12] 姥 read 木五切 mu.

[13] *Shih shuo hsin yü* 2B. 40b-41a: 王平子年十四五，見王夷甫婦郭氏貪，欲令婢路上儋糞 平子諫之，並言不可．郭大怒，謂平子曰：昔夫人臨終，以小郎囑新婦，不以新婦囑小郎． *Hsin fu* literally means "the bride."

[14] *Shu I* 1. 12a.

[15] This is used chiefly in southeast China, as in Kiangsu, Kwangtung, etc. It literally means "the old male."

[16] A very common term used in the sense of "husband"; literally, "male."

[17] *Shih ching* 3C. 3a: 士.

[18] 伯; see p. 193, note 80.

[19] *Shih ching* 4C. 2b: 子.

[20] *Ibid.* 7A. 5a.

[21] *Mêng Tzŭ* 6A. 4a; *Hou Han Shu* 113. 9.

[22] *Kuo Yü* 6. 8b; *Mêng Tzŭ* 6A. 6a.

not be determined. They might be merely general complimentary terms for man used in the sense of "husband," or simply circumlocutory expressions. T'ien,[23] so t'ien,[24] and kao chên [25] are primarily literary forms; kao chên is used almost exclusively in poetry.

The wife calls the husband liang,[26] liang jên,[27] lang,[28] and ch'ing.[29] Ch'in is a common reciprocal term. All these words are old forms, now chiefly retained in literary usage and seldom, if ever, used in the vocative. The wife may call the husband by his personal name, or just "you,"[30] and most prevalently she employs teknonymy.

The depreciatory terms are wai tzǔ,[31] and cho fu 拙夫 or yü fu 愚夫. These terms are employed only in refined society. Ordinarily, the wife refers to her husband as t'a 他, meaning "he" or "him," or by teknonymous and circumlocutory expressions.

Huang p'i [32] is an ancient and now obsolete posthumous term.

5. Po 伯 h o b

Hsiung kung is used in the Êrh Ya. Kung 公 is often written 伀 or 妐, and is sometimes pronounced chung.[33] Hsiung chang [34] was commonly used during the Han period. Chang is written 倬 or 嫜.

Po means principally father's older brother. Its extension to husband's older brother first occurred at about the end of the T'ang period.[35] This change can be explained on the basis of teknonymy. Po po is more colloquial.

[23] I Li 30.15b. T'ien (heaven) is used in the sense of the "positive" or "male" principle.
[24] 所天 is based on the above, employed only in literary usages, i. e., non-vocative and non-referential.
[25] 古絕句四首 [Yü t'ai hsin yung chi 10.6a]: 藁砧.
[26] I Li 5.8a.
[27] Shih ching 6C.8a; Mêng Tzǔ 8B.11b-12a.
[28] Chin shu 96.9b.
[29] Shih shuo hsin yü 3B.48b-49a: 卿.
[30] Yen shih chia hsün 1.13b: 倡和之禮，或爾汝之。
[31] Wife calls husband wai and husband calls wife nei; this practice dates from the middle of the first millennium A.D. Cf. Hêng Yen Lu 3.11a.
[32] Li Chi 5.22a: 皇辟.   [33] Êrh Ya commentary.   [34] Shih Ming: 兄章.
[35] See p. 193, note 81.

6. Mu mu 母母 h o b w

Ssŭ fu is the ancient term used in the *Êrh Ya*,[36] and is scarcely known today. *Mu mu* first came into use during the Sung period.[37] It is sometimes written 姆姆; the pronunciation differs slightly in different localities.

7. Shu 叔 h y b

Hsiao shu,[38] *shu lang*,[39] and *hsiao lang*[40] are alternative terms that date from the fourth and fifth centuries A. D. *Hsiao shu* is more colloquial, *shu lang* and *hsiao lang* are more literary. *Shu* is used in the *Êrh Ya*.

In the lower strata of present-day society, the younger brother-in-law can usually " play jokes " with the older sister-in-law. This circumstance is primarily based on the popular assumption that the younger brother-in-law is always a minor and that the older sister-in-law assumes a kind of maternal attitude.

8. Shên shên 嬸嬸 h y b w

Ti fu is an ancient term.[41] *Ssŭ* and *ti* are also used in the *Êrh Ya* to mean sisters who married the same man; the younger calls the older *ssŭ*, and the older calls the younger *ti*.[42] This usage is probably connected with the *yin* marriage. When used for husband's brother's wives, the *fu* should be appended as it is in the *Êrh Ya* and *I Li* (33. 2a-b).

Shên shên was first used during the Sung period.[43] *Shên* was originally a term for father's younger brother's wife, and its extension to husband's younger brother's wife is certainly teknonymous.

Female ego and husband's brothers' wives may refer to each other as *ti ssŭ*, as recorded in the *Êrh Ya*, and as *hsien hou*[44] and *chou li*,[45] as used during the Han period. *Ti ssŭ* and *hsien hou*

---

[36] 姒婦.
[37] See p. 201, note 104.
[38] *Shih Chi* 69. 15b-16a.
[39] *Wên Hsüan* 40. 6b.
[40] *Chin Shu* 96. 9b.
[41] Cf. *Êrh ya.*
[42] 姒, 娣.
[43] See p. 201, notes 103, 104.
[44] *Han Shu* 25A. 18b: 先後.
[45] *Fang Yen* 12. 1a: 築娌. *Chu* is a synonym of 妯.

are now obsolete. *Chu li* is the prevailing term at present; it is reciprocal and used only in the referential.

9. Ku 姑 h si

Ta ku 大姑 may be used for the older sister, and *hsiao ku* 小姑 for the younger sister, of the husband. On the other hand, *ta ku* need not necessarily indicate that the sister is actually older than the husband, since the female siblings may be counted in a separate numerical series. Hence *ta* and *hsiao* may only indicate the seniority and juniority among the husband's female siblings. In fact, *ta ku* and *hsiao ku* may be both younger than the husband. These terms are mainly used for the husband's unmarried sisters, but they may continue to be used after their marriage, though rarely.

In the *Êrh Ya*, husband's older sister is called *nü kung* 女公, and the younger, *nü mei* 女妹. *Shu mei* was used during the Han period.[46] *Hsiao ku* was first applied ca. the fifth century A.D. Since *ku* originally meant father's sister, its extension is attributable to teknonymy.

10. Ku fu 姑夫 h si h

Ku fu also means father's sister's husband, and its application to husband's sister's husband is undoubtedly teknonymous.

---

[46] Cf. *Hou Han Shu* 114. 8.

CONCLUSIONS

Having discussed the system in its morphological and historical aspects, I shall here venture upon a few concluding remarks. It may safely be asserted that during the last two thousand years the system has undergone a series of changes both in its structural principles and terminological categories, yet has retained many features of the old system. The latter stability seems to be related to the continuity of Chinese civilization as a whole. As regards the changes, there is, generally speaking, a broad historical correlation with the changes in the development of Chinese society. One notes that practically all the kinship changes occurred during the last two centuries of the first millennium B. C. and the whole of the first millennium A. D. During this period the system was in a state of flux. Many old terms were dropped, changed, or delimited in connotation. New terms were introduced, as if by way of experiment; some were incorporated into the system, others fell into oblivion. Almost all the new terms used in the modern system originated at this time. The whole system was finally stabilized during the T'ang period, after a thousand years of constant transformation and confusion.

This millennium likewise was a period of civil and social strife, the aftermath of the dissolution of the old feudal system. To be sure, the entire social structure was not suddenly transformed; many of the old social institutions lingered on, though in slightly modified forms.[1] Nevertheless, the evolution of the new social order was begun. It was a slow and gigantic process, accompanied by periods of alternating political and social tranquillity and chaos, of reactionary and progressive thought. This was an age of widening contacts with outside influences, especially from the third to the sixth centuries A. D., the "Dark Ages" of Chinese history, when nearly all the territory north of the Yangtze was overrun by less civilized peoples from the northern steppes; the resultant

[1] There are students who would even consider present China a fundamentally feudal society. This is somewhat an exaggeration and depends on one's definition of "feudalism."

large waves of Chinese migration southward resulted in the efflorescence of the *shih tsu* 世族 organization and its excrescent manifestation in the *mên fa* 門閥 [2] system of official recruitment. The entire process is too complex a subject to be dealt with here, but it shows a general chronological correlation with the development of the kinship system. When the kinship system crystalized toward the end of the first millennium A. D., Chinese society still continued to evolve. The kinship system, being a more conservative institution and in some ways a stabilizing mechanism for other social institutions, has remained essentially the same as it was during the T'ang period.

The individual parts of the system have exhibited varying amounts and rates of change, i. e., the changes have been differential. The nomenclature for sib relatives has experienced relatively little alteration, although there have been refinements in the degrees of differentiation and, for some terms, changed connotations. This may be due to the fact that, although the old sib system, *tsung fa*, has been transformed into the modern sib organization, *shih tsu*, the sib principle has remained the basis of kinship evolution. The increased descriptive efficacy represents merely refinements of superficial features of the system, correlated with the elaboration of the mourning ritualism.

Most remarkable changes have occurred in the terminology for non-sib relatives, especially in the nomenclature for affinal relatives, which Aginsky calls "basic terminology." [3] A glance at Tables III and IV will show how radical and complete the changes are. It is a generally accepted fact among social anthropologists that the affinal terminology is extremely sensitive to variations in marital relationships. But have the Chinese marriage regulations radically changed during this period? This question finds a simple answer in history. The most important factor in the regulation of marriage in China, from the first millennium B. C. down to the present, has been sib-exogamy supplemented by the genera-

[2] *Mên fa*, as a system of official recruitment, is based on sib connections. Cf. 楊筠如: 九品中正與六朝門閥 [1931].

[3] B. W. AGINSKY: Kinship systems and the forms of marriage, *Memoirs, American Anthropological Association*, 45 (1935), 14.

tion principle. It has been pointed out above that as time went on a gradual stiffening of this rule took place, but there was little actual change. In general, the effect of marriage regulations upon the kinship system has been so small that we are justified in ignoring it. We can also, in the manner employed before, dispose of the sororate and the levirate as moulding influences on the system.

Cross-cousin marriage, however, presents a very different problem, for it is upon this that the affinal terminology of the old system was undoubtedly based. If we assume that the decline in the frequency of this form of marriage resulted in the breakdown of the old affinal nomenclature, we must still explain the origin of the new terminology. These new terms are, in my opinion, not the products of new forms of marriage, but are the result of the operation of teknonymy. Marital relationships as a whole have had little influence upon the modern system. The reason for this may lie in the fact that the Chinese marriage regulations are purely restrictive, not prescriptive, i. e., aside from certain restrictions connected with sib-exogamy and generation, there is complete freedom of choice.

The morphological configuration of the Chinese sytem has puzzled many a student. Morgan, in generalizing on the system, vacillated between his Malayan and Turanian, saying that "it falls below the highest type of the Turanian form, and affiliates wherever it diverges with the Malayan." [4] Lowie, apparently using the same material, considered the Chinese system either a "generation" or a "bifurcate merging" system [5]—which is equivalent to saying that it is either Malayan or Turanian. T. S. Chen and J. K. Shryock, using Lowie's system of classification, call the Chinese system "bifurcate collateral." [6] Kroeber is of the same opinion, but says, "the Chinese system appears to consist of a 'classificatory,' that is non-descriptive, base, which has been made over by additions into a 'descriptive' system similar in its working to the English one, in fact is more precisely and successfully

[4] MORGAN: *System* . . . , *op. cit.*, 413.
[5] R. H. LOWIE: Relationship Terms, *Encyclopaedia Britannica*[12].
[6] *Op. cit.*, 627.

descriptive than this."[7] Compare this with Morgan's remark that the Chinese system " has accomplished the difficult task of maintaining a principle of classification which confronts the natural distinctions in the relationships of consanguinei, and, at the same time, of separating those relationships from each other in a precise and definite manner."[8]

Actually, the Chinese system is not one that lends itself to any simple characterization in terms such as "classificatory" or "descriptive." It must first be understood in the light of its own morphological principles and historical development. In Morgan's definition of the terms, the Chinese system is both classificatory and descriptive. This is not an "inconsistency" from the point of view of Morgan's system, but a characteristic of a system moulded by diverse factors of a counteracting nature. It is the elucidation of these underlying factors that is of scientific import rather than any particular characterization. This problem has been approached through a detailed analysis of the changes which the Chinese system has undergone during the documentary period of its history. Insofar as the data have permitted, correlative sociological facts have been evaluated with reference to these changes and the nature of possible dynamic factors indicated.

---

[7] Process in the Chinese Kinship, *op. cit.*, 151.
[8] MORGAN: *Systems* . . . , 413.

CHINESE WORKS FREQUENTLY CITED

The following list has been prepared for the sole purpose of avoiding the constant repetition of bibliographical information in the text. The works are arranged alphabetically according to the romanized brief title as used in the text and notes. Since full bibliographical information is usually given in the notes for Chinese works cited only once or twice and for European works referred to, they are not given here.

Chan kuo ts'ê 戰國策校注: commentaries by Pao Piao 鮑彪, circa 1150 A.D., and Wu Shih-tao 吳師道, 1283-1344 A.D.; Ssŭ pu ts'ung k'an 四部叢刊.

Ch'ang li chi 昌黎先生集: Collected works of Han Yü 韓愈, 768-824 A.D.; Ssŭ pu pei yao 四部備要.

Ch'ao ching ch'ao wên chi 巢經巢文集: Collected works of Chêng Chên 鄭珍, 1806-1864 A.D.; 清代學術叢書 edition.

Ch'êng wei lu 稱謂錄: by Liang Chang-chü 梁章鉅, 1775-1849 A.D.; 1875 edition.

Chêng tzŭ t'ung 正字通: compiled circa 1670 A.D. by Liao Wên-ying 廖文英; 1670 edition.

Chi yün 集韻: compiled by Ting Tu 丁度, 990-1053 A.D., and others; Ssŭ pu pei yao edition.

Chiang Wên-t'ung chi 江文通集: Collected works of Chiang Yen 江淹, 444-505 A.D.; Ssŭ pu ts'ung k'an edition.

Ch'ien yen t'ang chin shih wên pa wei 潛研堂金石文跋尾: by Ch'ien Ta-hsin 錢大昕, 1727-1804 A.D.; 1884 潛研堂全書 edition.

Chin shih li 金石例: by P'an Ang-hsiao 潘昂霄, circa 1300 A.D.; 徐氏隨菴叢書 edition.

Chin shih ts'ui pien 金石萃編: compiled by Wang Ch'ang 王昶, 1727-1806 A.D.; 經訓堂 edition.

Chin shih yao li 金石要例: by Huang Tsung-hsi 黃宗羲, 1609-1695 A.D.; 借月山房彙鈔 edition.

Chin shu 晉書: by Fang Chiao 房喬, circa 630 A.D., and others; 1894, 同文書局 edition.

Ch'in shu chi 親屬記: by Chêng Chên 鄭珍, 1806-1864 A.D.; 廣雅叢書 edition.

CHINESE WORKS FREQUENTLY CITED 131

Chiu T'ang shu 舊唐書: by Liu Hsü 劉昫, 887-946 A. D., and others; 1894, 同文書局 edition.

Ch'ü-chiang wên chi 曲江文集: Collected works of Chang Chiu-ling 張九齡, 673-740 A. D.; *Ssŭ pu ts'ung k'an* edition.

Êrh ya 爾雅義疏: Commentary by Ho I-hsing 郝懿行, 1757-1825 A. D.; *Ssŭ pu pei yao* edition. Since the section referred to is the short *Shih Ch'in* 釋親, Relationship Terms, no page reference is given in the notes.

Fang yen 方言: by Yang Hsiung 揚雄, 53 B. C.-18 A. D.; commentary by Kuo P'o 郭璞, 276-324 A. D.; *Ssŭ pu ts'ung k'an* edition.

Han fei tzŭ 韓非子: by Han Fei 韓非, ?-324 B. C.; *Ssŭ pu pei yao* edition.

Han shu 漢書: by Pan Ku 班固, 32-92 A. D.; 1894, 同文書局 edition.

Hêng yen lu 恆言錄: by Ch'ien Ta-hsin 錢大昕, 1727-1804 A. D.; 1884, 潛研堂全書 edition.

Hou Han shu 後漢書: by Fan Yeh 范曄, ?-445 A. D.; 1894, 同文書局 edition.

Hsiao ching 孝經注疏: 115, 阮刻十三經注疏 edition.

Hsin shu 新書: by Chia I 賈誼, *circa* second century B. C.; *Ssŭ pu pei yao* edition.

Hsin T'ang shu 新唐書: by Ou-yang Hsiu 歐陽修, 1007-1072 A. D., and Sung Ch'i 宋祁, 998-1061 A. D.; 1894, 同文書局 edition.

Hsüeh lin 學林: by Wang Kuan-kuo 王觀國, *circa* 1140 A. D.; 武英殿聚珍版 edition.

Hua yang chi 華陽集: by Ku K'uang 顧況, *circa* 8th and 9th centuries A. D.; 1855 雙峰堂 edition.

Huai nan tzŭ 淮南子: attributed to Liu An 劉安, ?-122 B. C.; 1876 浙江書局 edition.

I ching 周易注疏: 1815 阮刻十三經注疏 edition.

I li 儀禮注疏: 1815 阮刻十三經注疏 edition.

Jih chih lu 日知錄集釋: by Ku Yen-wu 顧炎武, 1612-1681 A. D., commentary by Huany Ju-ch'êng 黃汝成; 1872 湖北崇文書局 edition.

Jung chai sui pi 容齋隨筆: by Hung Mai 洪邁, 1123-1202 A.D.; *Ssŭ pu ts'ung k'an* 續編 edition.

Kai yü ts'ung k'ao 陔餘叢考: by Chao I 趙翼, 1727-1814 A.D.; 1790, 壽考堂甌北全書 edition.

Kuang shih ch'in 廣釋親: by Chang Shên-i 張愼儀, based on 錢塘梁氏殘藁. 變園叢書 edition.

Kuang ya 廣雅疏證: by Chang I 張揖, circa 230 A.D., commentary by Wang Nien-sun 王念孫, 1744-1832 A.D.; 1879, 淮南書局 edition. Since the section referred to is the *Shih Ch'in* 釋親, Relationship Terms, 6.1-6, no page reference is given in the notes.

Kuang yün 廣韻: revised by Ch'ên P'êng-nien 陳彭年, 961-1017 A.D., and others; *Ssŭ pu ts'ung k'an* edition.

Kung-yang chuan 公羊注疏: 1815, 阮刻十三經注疏 edition.

K'ung ts'ung tzŭ 孔叢子: attributed to K'ung Fu 孔鮒, circa 200 B.C.; *Ssŭ pu ts'ung k'an edition.*

Kuo yü 國語: commentary by Wei Chao 韋昭, 204-273 A.D.; *Ssŭ pu ts'ung k'an* edition.

Li chi 禮記注疏: 1815 阮刻十三經注疏 edition.

Liang shu 梁書: by Yao Ssŭ-lien 姚思廉, ?-637 A.D.; 1894 同文書局 edition.

Liu Pin-k'o wên chi 劉賓客文集: Collected works of Liu Yü-hsi 劉禹錫, 772-842 A.D.; *Ssŭ pu pei yao* edition.

Lu Shih-lung wên chi 陸士龍文集: Collected works of Lu Yün 陸雲, 262-305 A.D.; *Ssŭ pu ts'ung k'an* edition.

Lun yü 論語注疏: 1815, 阮刻十三經注疏 edition.

Lü shih ch'un ch'iu 呂氏春秋: attributed to Lü Pu-wei 呂不韋, ?-235 B.C.; *Ssŭ pu pei yao* edition.

Mêng ch'i pi t'an 夢溪筆談: by Shên Kua 沈括, 1030-1094 A.D.; 津逮秘書 edition.

Mêng tzŭ 孟子注疏: 1815 阮刻十三經注疏 edition.

Ming lü chi chieh fu li 明律集解附例: compilation of 1585 A.D., 萬曆十三年; 1908, 修定法律館 edition.

Ming tao tsa chih 明道雜志: by Chang Lei 張耒, 1052-1112 A.D.; 顧氏文房小說 edition.

Mo chi 默記: by Wang Chih 王銍, circa 1120 A.D.; 1918 涵芬樓 edition.

Nan shih 南史: by Li Yen-shou 李延壽, circa seventh century A. D.; 1894 同文書局 edition.

Nan T'ang shu 南唐書: by Ma Ling 馬令 circa 1100 A. D.; Ssŭ pu ts'ung k'an 續編 edition.

Nêng kai chai man lu 能改齋漫錄: by Wu Tsêng 吳曾, circa 1150 A. D.; 武英殿聚珍版 edition.

Pa ch'iung shih chin shih pu chêng 八瓊室金石補正: compiled by Lu Tsêng-hsiang 陸增祥, circa 1850 A. D.; 吳興劉氏希古樓 edition.

Pai ching t'ang wên chi 拜經堂文集: by Tsang Yung 臧庸, 1767-1811 A. D.;1920 上元宗氏石印 edition.

Pai hu t'ung 白虎通疏證: attributed to Pan Ku 班固, 32-92 A. D., and others; commentary by Ch'ên Li 陳立, 1809-1869 A. D.; 1875 淮南書局 edition.

Pei Ch'i shu 北齊書: by Li Pai-yao 李百藥, 565-648 A. D.; 1894 同文書局 edition.

Pei mêng so yen 北夢瑣言: by Sun Kuang-hsien 孫光憲, ?-968 A. D.; 雅雨堂叢書 edition.

Pei shih 北史: by Li Yen-shou 李延壽, circa 7th century A. D.; 1894 同文書局 edition.

P'ieh chi 瞥記: by Liang Yü-shêng 梁玉繩, circa 1780 A. D.; 清白士集 edition.

San kuo chih 三國志: by Ch'ên Shou 陳壽, 233-297 A. D.; 1894 同文書局 edition.

Shih ch'ang t'an 釋常談: anonymous; circa 1100 A. D.; 百川學海 edition.

Shih chi 史記: by Ssŭ-ma Ch'ien 司馬遷, ?145-74? B. C.; 1894 同文書局 edition.

Shih ching 毛詩注疏: Ssŭ pu pei yao edition.

Shih ming 釋名疏證: by Liu Hsi 劉熙, circa 200 A. D., commentary by Pi Yüan 畢沅, 1730-1797 A. D.; 廣雅叢書 edition. The part referred to is the Section II: Shih Ch'in Shu 釋親屬, Relationship Terms. No page reference is given in the notes.

Shih shuo hsin yü 世說新語: by Liu I-ch'ing 劉義慶, 403-444 A. D., commentary by Liu Hsiao-piao 劉孝標, circa 530 A. D.; Ssŭ pu ts'ung k'an edition.

Shu ching 尙書注疏: 1815, 阮刻十三經注疏 edition.
Shu i 書儀:by Ssŭ-ma Kuang 司馬光, 1019-1086 A.D.; 學津討原 edition.
Shu p'o 鼠璞: by Tai Shih 戴埴, circa 1220 A.D.; 學津討原 edition.
Shuo wên 說文解字: by Hsü Shên 許愼, circa 200 A.D., commentary by Hsü Hsüan 徐鉉, 916-991 A.D.; Ssŭ pu ts'ung k'an edition.
Sung shu 宋書: by Shên Yo 沈約, 441-513 A.D.; 1894 同文書局 edition.
Ta Tai li chi 大戴禮記: by Tai Tê 戴德, circa 100 B.C.; Ssŭ pu ts'ung k'an edition.
T'ang chih yen 唐摭言: by Wang Ting-pao 王定保, 870-954 (?) A.D.; 雨雅堂叢書 edition.
T'ang lü su i 故唐律疏議: codified by Ch'ang-sun Wu-chi 長孫無忌, ?-659 A.D. and others. Ssŭ pu ts'ung k'an 三編 edition.
Ts'ai Chung-lang chi 蔡中郎集: Collected works of Ts'ai Yung 蔡邕, 133-192 A.D.; Ssŭ pu ts'ung k'an edition.
Ts'ao Tzŭ-chien chi 曹子建集: Collected works of Ts'ao Chih 曹植, 192-232 A.D.; Ssŭ pu ts'ung k'an edition.
Tso chuan 左傳注疏: 1815, 阮刻十三經注疏 edition.
Tsung fa hsiao chi 宗法小記: by Ch'êng Yao-t'ien 程瑤田, 1725-1814 A.D.; 清經解 edition.
T'ung su p'ien 通俗篇: by Chai Hao 翟灝, ?-1788 A.D.; 無不宜齋 edition.
T'ung tien 通典: compiled by Tu Yu 杜佑, 735-812 A.D.; 1896, 浙江書局 edition.
T'ung ya 通雅: by Fang I-chih 方以智, circa 1650 A.D.; 立教館 edition.
Wang Shih-chung chi 王侍中集: Collected works of Wang Ts'an 王粲, 177-217 A.D.; 漢魏六朝百三名家集 edition.
Wei Wu-ti chi 魏武帝集: Collected works of Ts'ao Ts'ao 曹操, 155-220 A.D.; 漢魏六朝百三名家集 edition.
Wên hsüan 六臣註文選: compiled by Hsiao T'ung 蕭統, 501-531 531 A.D., commentary by Li Shan 李善, ?-688 A.D. and others. Ssŭ pu ts'ung k'an edition.

Yen shih chia hsün 顏氏家訓: by Yen Chih-t'ui 顏之推, 531-591 A. D.; *Ssŭ pu pei yao* edition.

Yen tzŭ ch'un ch'iu 晏子春秋: attributed to Yen Ying 晏嬰, ?-493 B. C.; *Ssŭ pu pei yao* edition.

Yin hua lu 因話錄: by Chao Lin 趙璘, *circa* 840 A. D.; 稗海 edition.

Yü p'ien 玉篇: compiled in 543 A. D. by Ku Yeh-wang 顧野王 augmented in 760 A. D. by Sun Ch'iang 孫強, revised in 1008 A. D. by Ch'ên P'êng-nien 陳彭年, and others; *Ssŭ pu ts'ung k'an* edition.

Yü t'ai hsin yung chi 玉臺新詠集: compiled by Hsü Ling 徐陵, 507-583 A. D.; *Ssŭ pu ts'ung k'an* edition.

Yüan shih chang-ch'ing chi 元氏長慶集: Collected works of Yüan Chên 元稹, 779-831 A. D.; *Ssŭ pu ts'ung k'an* edition.